YOUR INCREDIBLE ENERGY FIELD

creative pathway to health and happiness

by
Ronald Polack

other works

Book
Vibrational Vitality (Trafford Publishing)

Audiobook
The Human Energy Field (iTunes)

Cover photograph – Chris Harris – www.chrisharris.com
Cover design – KeyBoard Graphic Design – www.maddi.ca

Contact Information
info@ronald-healing.com

DEDICATED TO
each of our children

Andrew Brenda Dave Russ Rob

unique individuals who care for their
families, friends and associates with
genuineness and vibrant living

and

to June

wife, partner and dearest companion
inspires me through her living, never fails
to encourage me in my work, backed up
this book with hours of proof reading and
constructive critique

Table of Contents

Part One: Vibrational Healing

Energy!   1

Discovery   5

Personal Magnetism Revealed   11

The Rainbow of Your Invisible Spectrum   17

The 24/7 Genie   29

The Healing Charge   37

Cures are Rest-Stops Along the Way   45

Healing Experiences   53

Distance Healing   63

Is Dying Also Natural?   73

Social Survival   83

Part Two: Dynamics of Mind and Heart

Your Attitude   91

The Psyche of the Human Energy Field   99

Leaders, Gurus, Religion   111

New Levels of Perception   121

Instinct-Intuition-Insight   133

Individuation and the Soul's Code   141

Soft Listening and the Silent Mind   151

Epilogue   161

Bibliography   167

Part One:

Vibrational Healing

Energy!

There are many ways the word *energy* is defined and perhaps even more in the way that it is used. Examples:

- that person has good energy; I like her
- the music is energetic; so is my friend
- a source of useable power like electricity, fuel, horsepower, etc.
- simple physics – the capacity to do work

Currently there is considerable interest and promotion in what's called energy work or energy healing. It's almost a fad in alternative non-medical circles. Many therapists use a variety of commonplace or strange modalities under that name. I've often wondered what energy means to them or what ideas their patients might have about it. Is energy referring to a basic resource of vitality, strong or weak? Does a therapist have an excess of this vitality in his body that he, or she, can afford to pour it into a patient's body who seems to have less of it? If so, wouldn't the healer feel depleted after providing such an energy transfusion let alone how weak they might feel after treating a few people in a day? What a constant personal sacrifice that would be in the interest of someone else's health! Perhaps a treatment would involve some natural food or dietary supplement deemed to carry an exotic essence, energy, from a far-off source like the Amazon or a rediscovered magical ingredient from the ancient world.

Treatment is essentially a medical term of applying some substance that a sick person doesn't have, to alter their ill condition in a positive way. Treatment could cover surgery or medications to stimulate or retard a malfunction in a patient to help them feel better. Can one's energy be treated in this way? It's not my intention to criticize any physician or therapist for their chosen methods of treatment. Rather, the purpose of this book is to share my understanding of what Energy and Healing are to me and how they feature in my practice of assisting people back to physical health, emotional stability and optimum mental health.

The constant events involved in normal function of our human facilities are amazing and magical. I am always in awe of the coordinated intricacies of our hormonal, immune and nervous systems that trigger and monitor the functions of all our cells and organs, including the brain, to synchronize them so exactly and in a timely way that we hardly do more than "just enjoy" our healthy state, without even asking why. Perhaps even more fascinating is how massive re-calibrations jump into action during a sickness, accident or trauma, immediately initiating a re-balancing of thousands of chemical and physical interactions to return us to normal or at least a symptom-free state. I've always been asking the questions, "How does all that happen? What's behind it all? – that a human, animal or insect maintains the fullness of life in such a consistent way."

We know that we are not plugged into some power outlet like our homes and appliances or not tuned into some radiation like our cell phones. We may sense though that we are connected to some larger force that makes all this possible. That's where my curiosity led me to explore and eventually discover Human Energy Fields, perhaps more accurately called Human Electro-Magnetic Vibratory Fields. Over time some have called these invisible forces: life, spirit, bio-plasm, innate intelligence, divinity, God/Allah, etc. This book outlines my intention to explore in a down-to-earth way this long-forgotten Energy Field of ours that I call our greatest asset. Welcome to my journey!

Discovery

This book is about health and healing. First, let's discover our amazing hidden resources to achieve the mastery of vital and fulfilling lives. The first order of business is to acknowledge that each of us is maintained by what we might call a Bio-Energy Field or your Energy Field. You are not a machine! You never were a mechanical model lying inert on a factory assembly line waiting for millions of parts, cells, organs, systems to be created and fitted into you, like building an automobile. You are contained within your own active living Energy Field – an invisible cloak of life-giving energy coordinating all your parts. This Field was present when your parents conceived you, a creative Field guiding the development of your first body as it formed your embryo and of course after birth as you grew in stature. The Field's many vibrating frequencies dove-tail together so that you enjoy good health at all levels, mental emotional and physical. Your mind is not separate from your body, nor hormones from the nervous system, muscles from bone or thoughts from feelings. You are one, from the higher spiritual vibrations of your encircling Field to the lower vibrations affecting your amazing physical body. Separate you from your Field and you're a fish out of water, expiring quickly.

You are an individual right down to your DNA; your experiences from birth onward are uniquely yours. Some psychologists claim our pre-birth womb time is also individual and capable of being recalled. Your physical health is more than "feeling good" – in other words without symptoms. Health is the harmonious coordination of the trillions of cells that make up your body. Every cell in your body could be compared to each individual of the estimated seven billion people composing humankind with whom we share a common identity. Oneness – unified harmonious function or peace on earth – is theoretically present at the mass level but concepts and beliefs we hold individually separate us from that possibility. For example, we tend to make a big deal out of skin color, geography, language, culture, religion and personal viewpoints. Fear, greed and ambition motivate us to go to war to protect these differences or to snatch another country's resources, in spite of our common legacy as human beings. Similar motivations distort your personal Energy Field and fragment your experience.

This fragmentation is evident in all professions, including the medical. Physicians specialize in different parts of the body and devise therapies related to their own area of interest. It has been said, "Specialization is an attempt to learn more and more about less and less – this can result in knowing everything about nothing." There ought to be treatments that enhance a patient's whole body rather than just parts of it. Medical short-sightedness produces countless side effects in patients. A frightening number of patients suffer and die from *iatrogenic* illnesses – diagnostic and treatment mistakes by their doctors and their medical support teams. In the year 2000 alone, medication error was a leading cause of death in the U.S., according to a report by John Hopkins University to the Journal of the American Medical Association. Even so, the medical establishment, influenced by the pharmaceutical industry, belittles alternative or complementary health providers whose therapies are less invasive yet often are very effective. Alternative practitioners may describe themselves as holistic. But are they? If *holistic* refers to the wholeness of a human being, the primary consideration would be the Energy Field of their patient. How is the Field affected by any remedy or treatment, as well by the quality of communication between the patient and the therapist? The human mind is deemed the province of psychiatrists and psychologists, but after 150 years of psychotherapeutic advances has there actually been any improvement in the mental heath of the population? As for our spiritual health, the religious fraternity advocates we develop a relationship with a deity; in addition they demand our support through fear and shame. Their simple solution is to petition a higher power to assuage our miseries. Without doubt there are many well-intentioned doctors, ministers and therapists but their value is seriously limited if the living Field, our life-line, is not taken into account.

The clarity of the Energy Field's powerful presence is supremely important; however, as with our body and our mind it is susceptible to stress and trauma. Actually, it ought to be the first consideration in any analysis or therapy. Balance and clear the Field first. Then follow up, if necessary, with other procedures. On a rare occasion a practitioner skilled in Bio-Energy healing is present during a surgical operation. The result, as in my own experience, is that healing time is dramatically reduced as steps are taken to restore the Field during and after the trauma of an accident or surgery. A mental shock or emotional crisis will also traumatize the Field and lead to physical problems sooner or later. Your Field's ability to maintain balance, clarity and flow in your body will be hampered if you're stressed-out or over-fatigued. Inner conflict distorts your Field and undermines your health.

Vibrational Healing restores health. In my practice I stimulate my patient's Field, using my own Energy radiation. I feel the release of their blockages and imbalances. A patient's resilient Field, always responsive to a positive influence, will accept this healing charge restoring its integrity to regenerate the body. Then hormones rebalance, nerve networks regain their coordination, and the powerful immune system resumes its protective role.

Once symptoms ease and health begins to return, patients may feel the urge to talk about their lifestyles and to make changes in their own best interest. Healing is a two-way street between the Vibrational Healer and the patient. As one of the partners in the process, the patient is wise to relinquish negative attitudes. It is common sense to avoid situations certain to cause stress and trauma or learn how to handle those challenges without being affected negatively. It is valuable to adopt a regimen of nutritional food plus physical exercise. A brisk walk each day can do wonders. In spite of the stress and strain of modern living (impossible to completely avoid) people can preserve and enhance their health through periodic healing sessions. As a Vibrational Healing practitioner I influence the patient's Energy, assisting them to release accumulated tension. As a result their thinking improves and influences the manner in which they conduct their lives. Simply stated, Vibrational Healing is a natural way to regain health and experience a new perspective on life.

Our problems, difficulties, fears and anxieties are symptoms of personal fragmentation. We lack understanding and contact with our invisible guardian through the Human Energy Field. We are therefore vulnerable to the winds that blow in our circumstances and we fear what might be in store for us down the road. We take on the role of the victim rather than the victor. Life from that vantage point is more of a nightmare than an enjoyable journey. Your Energy Field is the healing wind beneath your wings. This book will inspire you to rise in the thermals of that wind. You will see with a clearer perspective and be amazed at the positive changes available in your experience.

Throughout the pages of this book I consider our natural magnetism, explore the functions of our personal Energy Fields and illustrate how our bodies are designed to work in magical ways. I discuss Vibrational Healing in depth, map the cycles of the healing journey and outline my practice of remote healing i.e. healing conducted across any distance. Our attitudes, conditioned by stresses, pressures and fears we all encounter, have a direct bearing on our Energy Field thus affecting our health. You and I can choose to change those effects. Join me to discover more about you and how you can learn to live fully to your greater satisfaction.

Personal Magnetism Revealed
electrical, magnetic and living fields

As a child my wife played with two wee magnetized Scottie dogs which to her exhibited magical powers. These toys miraculously clung to each other head to head, but would repel each other when placed head to tail. She also discovered that if she placed one dog on a table surface and the other under the table, both would move in unison. What she didn't know as a child was that little magnetic iron bars embedded in the dogs emitted lines of positive force (north) from one end and negative force (south) from the other. In my high school physics class we experimented with magnetic and electromagnetic fields. We scattered iron filings on a sheet of paper resting on a magnet and watched the filings quickly arrange themselves as if being ordered to follow the design of the magnet's force field. We also discovered that an electric current in a wire generates an electromagnetic force field capable of inducing a current in a wire nearby. That's why live wires are insulated. The force fields in both cases were invisible to our eyes, and still are.

Force fields are found everywhere

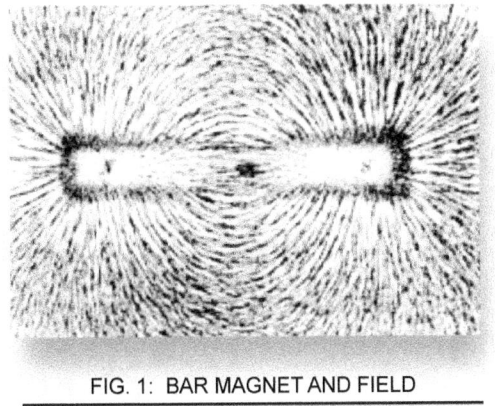

FIG. 1: BAR MAGNET AND FIELD

in nature. Consider the oak tree. It grew from a living seed carrying the blueprint of what was to come: the mature tree in all its splendor. The acorn you hold in your hand contains a living force field with all the wisdom necessary to create a tree under the right conditions. Amazing! When the acorn is surrounded by good soil, warmth and water and the force field carrying its design, a fledgling tree arises inch by inch – roots, trunk, branches, leaves and eventually more acorns. All living seeds like the acorn possess their own unique energy force fields containing electrical and magnetic properties. They overflow with life or bio; hence the term Bio-Energy-Field which also enables them to reproduce – a feat unavailable to the young girl's two magnetized Scottie dogs.

Let's investigate our physical bodies. Are they merely storehouses of thoughts, feelings, cells, organs and vital systems or is there something greater present? Can you envision yourself as an Energy Field much larger than your physical stature? Traditionally we believe our invisible life-giving essences are within us, as if enclosed in our flesh. And we support this belief with utterances such as "God or spirit is within us" or "our qualities are internal." Not quite accurate! Your Bio-Energy Field or Human Energy Field is an outside and an inside job. The Field is at a higher frequency than your body. It surrounds and penetrates you physically. It operates all your bodily functions at the unconscious level while making possible your thoughts and actions at the conscious level. At the moment of death the Field separates from the physical body, and the body loses all its living properties.

Western research probes further and further into our bodies microscopically to examine our DNA and genes which scientists say control who we are, what we think and do. That theory was called

"Genetic Determinism". Also through the modern religion of science we've discovered a host of microorganisms, bacteria and viruses which we blame for doing us in. Imagine what might be discovered by researching Human Energy Fields.

For example, do you know when your Field is blocked by negative influences? Probably not, but healing methods exist that can locate and release restrictions in your Field and free its powerful energies to your benefit. These could include the laying on of hands, prayer for healing, incantations from a witch doctor or remedies from a medicine man, all of which are regarded as non-scientific by most doctors and scientists. However these methods can enhance the condition of the Human Energy Field so that healing can occur. Some health professionals are more successful than others depending on a patient's openness and the therapist's perceptive ability to connect with their Energy Field. Some make that connection consciously, others unconsciously. It doesn't matter which way so long as the connection is made. A caring parent naturally has an empathic Energy connection with their child. Our two-year old son stuck his little finger inside a door jam as the door closed. Ouch! When freed, his finger resembled the letter Z. I held him on my knee, my arms around him, his injured hand in mine. He screamed in pain, then cried, then fell asleep. He awoke fifteen minutes later and to my surprise his finger looked normal although I was sure it was still tender. Apparently not, for he was soon on the floor moving his toy cars around without any evidence of pain.

It may seem unusual to think of yourself as a Bio-Energy Field in human form containing many invisible dimensions – thoughts, feelings, qualities of character, unique talents and self-healing powers. Until you express them they remain secrets, sometimes even to yourself.

Within your dimensions, both physical and invisible, are vibratory frequencies comparable to the rainbow spectrum within white light. The highest color frequency is violet, the lowest is red. Similarly, the physical body represents the lowest frequency, the mind a higher one. More subtle frequencies, higher yet, include extra-sensory perception (ESP). Even a soul frequency is present. When these levels blend, free of impediments, your Energy Field orchestrates harmonious interactions within your body, mind and emotions.

The electromagnetic properties of our Energy Fields are used in medical diagnostic procedures such as the electrocardiogram (ECG) and the magnetic resonance imaging machine (MRI). Scientists continue looking for other ways to usefully exploit our electromagnetic properties to enhance diagnosis and treatment. In his book, *Vibrational Medicine*, Richard Gerber, M.D., observes:

The current practice of medicine is based upon the Newtonian model of reality... The Einsteinian paradigm as applied to vibrational medicine sees human beings as networks of complex energy fields that interface with physical/cellular systems. Vibrational medicine uses specialized forms of energy to positively affect those energetic systems that may be out of balance due to disease states. By rebalancing the energy fields that help to regulate cellular physiology, vibrational healers attempt to restore order from a higher level of human functioning.

U.S. psychologist and physiologist Dr. Valerie Hunt in her book *Infinite Mind*, documents her years of research into human vibration patterns during pain, disease and illness. She writes:

Electromedical researchers believe that each disease or

functional disturbance has its own energy field which must be reversed before healing can take place. Probably illness is a disturbance first in the energy field and healing is the restoration of that field to health.

Indeed there is more to us than meets the eye. Over the past 50 years my patients have benefited from healing through their Energy Fields despite comments from others, "It can't be done!" or "It's not scientific!" Well it's interesting to note I'm not alone in my own little corner. Scientists working in cutting-edge quantum physics validate the Field's hidden potentials for healing, telepathy, intuition, etc. A new day is dawning as more people wake up to physical healing through the Bio-Energy Field. Also, by understanding our vibrational natures we will open doors to expand our mental and intuitive capabilities.

The Rainbow of Your Invisible Spectrum

In my chiropractic practice I used my hands to adjust misaligned vertebrae of the spinal column to relieve restrictions to nerve flow in spinal cord and spinal nerves. As more patients experienced a return to health, more people were attracted to my practice. Over time my partner and I discerned energy fields of patients and sensed energetic disturbances in the same areas we had located nerve pressure. We then became aware of life currents moving through our hands allowing us to eliminate their energy blockages without adjustments or manipulation. We were of course impressed and excited about the possibilities in this touch-without-force technique and used it as an alternative to physical adjustments. Awed by this discovery, I recognized I was touching into a powerful reservoir around each person – their Bio-Energy Field.

Your personal Energy Field, of which you may be unaware, affects the Fields of others – positively or negatively. Ever talk to a depressed or frustrated person then walk away feeling disturbed yourself? And later the discomfort could arise again when you bring the individual to mind. On the other hand, people who express a positive attitude and a sunny disposition make our day; they inspire and uplift us. Which only proves how closely connected we are with each other. Our temperaments, good or bad, influence those around us.

In his book *The Chakras* published in 1927, C.W. Leadbeater described and attached names to components of the invisible aura, the portion of the Human Energy Field capable of being seen by certain individuals. He called these components *chakras*, a name that originated in the Far East. His book included colored images drawn by clairvoyants who said they saw chakras. Specialized photography later captured auras on film to reveal variations in color depending on the emotional states of those being photographed. Other methods have since been developed to show the Fields of human beings and other life forms.

Western culture perceives our bodies as physical-chemical machines victimized by incoming bacteria, viruses, toxins and external stresses. So in order to protect us from these nasty invaders the medical/scientific community has swelled its medicine chest with a host of drugs and medical procedures. Science has developed antiseptic methods for food handling and has helped improve sanitation and medical practice, including administration of

FIG. 2: BIO-ENERGY FIELD

Artwork by June Polack

medications, artificial immunizations, antibiotics, and refined diagnostic procedures. We spend millions researching cures and treatments for our physical bodies yet are miserly in spending dollars to investigate our invisible non-physical dimensions where healing lives. Who in the scientific establishment is actually aware of Bio-Energy Fields and how their invisible activity plays a key role in maintaining health or setting the stage for disease? What causes a Field to be distorted and how does that interfere with vital functions in our bodies? How can a Field be cleared so that health is known again? Sadly, the medical-scientific community does not ask these questions, hence no research dollars. Some scientists at the risk of their reputations in medical-pharmaceutical circles, have leaped ahead of their peers by researching these invisible components – the Field, the life force, the memory, the power of intention, the human spirit, etc., all of which have been relatively unexplored.

Doctors and scientists generally ascribe to the mechanistic view of life. That is, the human body is mechanical and can therefore be completely explained by the laws of physics and chemistry. Though some doctors may treat their patients as machines, the fact is that patients don't act or react in mechanical ways. Each human being is a living organism of trillions of cells within a system of electro-magnetic frequencies, their own Human Energy Field, as described in the previous chapter, *Personal Magnetism Revealed*. We are somewhat like the famous Russian Doll – a series of identical ever-smaller colorful wooden dolls fitting together perfectly one inside the other. To use this analogy, your physical body, the lowest level of vibrational frequency, is the tiny "doll" in the center. Superimposed on it are other more subtle energy "dolls", beginning with the etheric layer, the one closest to our body and penetrating it. This layer rebuilds, balances and heals body structures and regulates thousands of physical-chemical processes in each instant. It is dominant when you are relaxed, when you laugh and when you sleep. If the etheric level is obstructed by stress or trauma your self-healing capabilities are limited. This physical-etheric interface is a close "hand in glove" relationship -- one vibratory level merging with the other at an ultra-microscopic level. At this level meridians/pathways channel the energy of chi or life force throughout your body inter-connecting your internal organs. Vibrational Healing enhances the etheric's healing ability.

The second larger "doll" is the astral layer, the next highest rate of vibration. It is the home of awareness, of consciousness and thinking. It affects your physical organism differently than etheric vibrations. For example, you use up physical resources when you think, express and are physically active. So when you hit the pillow at night the astral influence may recede to allow the etheric to do its thing – to recuperate the body.

The spirit-ego layer, the next highest vibration, produces self-consciousness or awareness. Thoughts and feelings come and go and you experience a sense of continuity and permanence one moment to the next. Memory is also here allowing us to perceive who we are, to choose and to think for ourselves. This layer also oversees both astral and etheric influences over our bodies – even though we're not conscious of it. Not all schools of thought define these levels in the same way. For example, Dr. Richard Gerber in his book, *Vibrational Medicine*, lists them as physical, etheric, astral, mental and causal.

Life is motion! Its dance is in full swing under your skin even when you're quiet and resting. Your heart pumps blood, sometimes at breakneck speed, through thousands of miles of flexible pulsing arteries and veins. When you shift position, say from standing to bending, your muscles automatically alternate between contraction and relaxation; they adapt to keep you balanced. The same balancing is in play when you walk. As you lean your body forward your leg and torso muscles stop you from keeling over and bring you back into balance. During any move from rest to action most of your blood volume shifts to your surface muscles. After eating, blood has gathered in the abdomen to assist in digestion and some say it's not a good idea to go swimming or running since you may experience cramps. Intricate hormonal concentrations in the blood constantly adjust to maintain overall balance while accommodating changing needs in the body. Your abdominal organs and glands, always in motion, dance their own unique rhythms. Alternating muscle contractions called *peristalsis* move material through the intestines. In the same way many glandular secretions are moved along narrow ducts or channels to their destinations. Millions of miles of nerve fibers host electric-like impulses flashing faster than the speed of light. Even when sedentary, your body performs miraculously. Imagine the accelerated artistry during more athletic activity when incredible strength, flexibility and stamina reveal how well our Energy Fields coordinate our bodies' ability to adapt.

Life's motion within the Bio-Energy Field is even more intense as constantly moving streams of energy are created by swirling, spinning chakras. The chakras are to the Human Energy Field what waves are to the ocean. They are power centers within the Field; they integrate the influences of the vibratory levels and transmit them to the physical body – remember those Russian Dolls you were introduced to earlier? Carolyn Myss in *Why People Don't Heal and How They Can*, writes:

For those in the West who are unfamiliar with Eastern terminology and metaphysics, it may be simpler to think of the chakras as computer disks that are imprinted with information of all sorts. Much like the hard disk in your computer, the chakras spin and take in data and also can be tapped to disgorge the same information. Each energy data bank resonates to a very specific vibration of energy needed by your physical and spiritual body.

The chakras exchange power and control between the Field and the physical body. Your body is strongly connected to your Bio-Energy Field by more than 30 chakras. 7 of them are designated major chakras, each having positions in the body strategic to nerve plexuses and hormone centers. Each major chakra influences many physical functions as well as having psychological and spiritual implications. For example, the heart chakra in the chest area influences breathing and cardiac rhythms that nourish and cleanse every cell of the body. Poets also describe the heart as a source of powerful emotion, the seat of love, joy

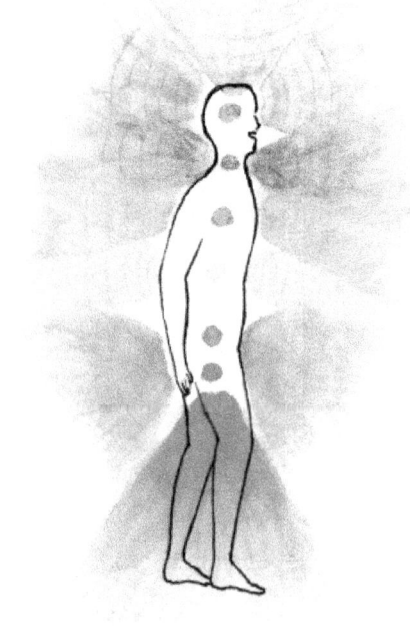

FIG. 3: CHAKRAS

Artwork by June Polack

and tenderness.

Chakras are often listed by number and by the color relative to their specific wave-length, for example:

> **Root chakra – red**
>
> **Pelvic chakra – orange**
>
> **Solar chakra – yellow**
>
> **Heart chakra – green**
>
> **Throat chakra – blue**
>
> **Brow/face chakra – indigo**
>
> **Crown chakra – purple/violet**

ROOT CHAKRA

The vortex of this energy located near the base of the pelvis is the Field's vibratory foundation. It spirals downward toward the feet and locks in with the Earth's vibration; it is our root to the planet and the family of humankind. Yoga practitioners believe the root chakra is the source of Kundalini, an intense spiritual experience of energy pulsing from this chakra to the crown chakra at the top of the head; they see it as a step toward enlightenment.

PELVIC CHAKRA

This chakra, penetrating the pelvis is located near a large nerve plexus. Physical function in this area includes absorbing fluid from digestive residue as it travels through the lower intestines called the bowel. Lucky for us; if the fluid introduced into the upper digestive tract is not reclaimed and recycled through lymphatic vessels and kidneys we'd be seriously dehydrated. The pelvic chakra also directly influences the reproductive organs whose powerful hormones

– estrogen from the ovaries and testosterone from the testes – affect the structure and function of the male and female gonads as well as secondary characteristics in the body such as hair distribution, shape of breasts and pelvis, and our mental/emotional make-up. It's no wonder we experience a sense of personal power when this chakra enlivens pelvic organs and glands. It also strengthens the lower spine and pelvis and is the attractive force behind relationships, sexuality, the longing for a sense of community and the desire for ritual in our lives.

SOLAR CHAKRA

It co-exists with the well-known solar plexus, a nerve network located above the waist and just below the rib cage. Here a delicate, powerful hormone balance fluctuates between adrenaline and insulin regulating blood sugar levels. Digestion in the stomach and small intestine is activated by acid and enzymes secreted by the stomach's lining, and by secretions from the pancreas and a flow of bile from the liver. Thus the complex chemical structure of foods that we eat is simplified so that their nutritive value can be absorbed to benefit our whole body. Up-tight unresolved emotions, commonly held in this area, can cause indigestion/reflux by obstructing solar chakra energy flow. Deep breathing and Vibrational Healing free the flow of energy to improve digestive efficiency. The solar chakra imbues us with a sense of self-esteem plus intestinal fortitude, popularly known as "guts", to achieve our highest intentions.

HEART CHAKRA

The body is connected to its environment by the heart chakra influencing the synchronized rhythms of breathing and cardiac function. These rhythms discharge waste gases from the lungs and distribute incoming oxygen to every cell via blood circulation. The thymus gland, a key organ in the immune system protecting us from invasive infectious elements, is located within the heart chakra field. The green richness of this chakra provides a foundation for our emotional health since it affects many of our vital functions. Here is where tender emotions of love and joy reside; the wellspring of love for self and compassion for others.

THROAT CHAKRA

The throat chakra surrounds thousands of connections moving between head and body – blood vascular, lymphatic, nerves, and flowing hormonal secretions. Hormones from the thyroid gland located in this area affect our metabolism, the rate at which our body uses energy. Parathyroid gland secretions balance the vital calcium content within each cell of the body. Of course the throat chakra permeates your larynx to produce a voice as individual to you as a fingerprint; it's purpose is communication – ultimately self expression.

BROW/FACE CHAKRA

The brow or face chakra is often called the Third Eye suggesting intuitive spiritual perception. The powerful senses of sight, hearing, taste and smell are within its purview. This particular area contains the threefold center of body control – pineal and pituitary glands within the brain structure and hypothalamus of the brain stem. The brain, recently recognized as a gland, secretes more than 3 dozen hormones thereby being both a hormonal and neurological center coordinating bodily functions.

CROWN CHAKRA

This crown of energy, encircling the top of your head, is a bridge between your individual Energy Field and the overall Human Energy Field in which we all find ourselves. The crown charka in cooperation with the heart chakra integrates your entire Bio-Energy system. Cerebrospinal fluid produced in the brain surrounds the brain and spinal cord and transmits an electro-magnetic pulse through the body via the whole nervous system. In *Why People Don't Heal and How They Can*, Carolyn Myss refers to the crown chakra as a spiritual bank account – an endless flow of grace, wisdom and guidance.

The preceding descriptions do little more than scratch the surface of chakra power centers. Ultimately we'll learn more about the Human Energy Field's intricate make-up. Although we cannot see an invisible Field, it nevertheless strongly influences our behavior and our experience in much the same way our invisible minds and emotions affect us. The Unknown challenges us to explore further, intuitively and scientifically.

The 24/7 Genie
always on the job!

Let's look at how our body operates. It is certainly animated physically with an alert mind, colorful emotions, memory and intuitive perception. And we have imagination – allowing us us to be in the present, past, or dreaming of the future – a creative facility when rightly used. Fortunately we are not aware of the magnitude of our operational systems keeping us alive or we'd be forever trying to adjust our heart rhythm, body temperature, etc. Would you know how to digest a ham sandwich and distribute the nutritional elements throughout your body? Imagine the time it would take to monitor all these processes, even if we knew how. But we each carry an innate wisdom I'm calling the *Genie*. The Genie manages the physical plant in which we live as we follow our whims and fancies, wisely or foolishly. Our state of health is determined by the extent we harmonize with the resident Genie within our Bio-Energy Field.

My college studies of anatomy, physiology, psychology and biochemistry were amazing discoveries, impeded only by the volume of information to be integrated in the short period of four years. Fortunately a balancing factor to "head learning" was the time spent developing hand-perception skills necessary for a chiropractor. A great deal of practice, much of it on each other, taught us to recognize physical normalities and distortions especially in spinal columns, limbs, and joints. We dissected cadavers and worked in a microbiology lab. As interns we diagnosed and treated people in an out-patient clinic. Through reading textbooks and dissecting cadavers we were introduced to intricate systems operating beneath our skins. For instance, trillions of cells, each an individual organism, take in oxygen and drive out gaseous wastes such as carbon dioxide.

Our lungs are two masses of delicate tissue so convoluted in design that their surface if stretched out would cover an area the size of a tennis court. Massive networks of capillaries (tiny thin-walled blood vessels) line the lungs' inner surfaces. The walls of these capillaries are thin enough to absorb by osmosis vital gases from the inhaled air and release waste gases to be exhaled. The lungs are inflated within the chest cavity by varying air pressures. Chest muscles raise, spread and alternately contract the rib cage. Larger muscles in the abdominal wall contract to push the diaphragm (a muscular tendon which separates chest and abdominal cavities) into a dome shape forcing air to be expelled from the lungs. As these sets of muscles relax, the diaphragm flattens to produce negative air pressure in the lungs, passively but forcibly drawing in fresh air. Incoming air is conditioned in our nasal and throat channels adjusting its humidity and temperature before it contacts the warm moist lining of the lungs. Otherwise extreme temperatures or dryness would damage delicate lung tissue.

The heart muscle's right side contracts after receiving returning blood from the body, sending the recycled fluid to fill the lungs' capillaries where the chemical/gas exchange takes place. Negative hydraulic pressure returns the oxygenated blood to the left side of the heart. Another contraction propels this vital fluid into the body's circulatory network via the aorta, the main trunk. Our bodies are home to thousands of miles of blood vessels; arteries distribute fresh oxygenated blood, veins draw the used blood back to the heart. Hemoglobin in red blood cells helps hold and distribute oxygen throughout our systems. A derivative of iron, hemoglobin is manufactured in the liver and is a key ingredient for building red cells in bone marrow and spleen. Each cubic millimeter of blood contains up to 6 million red blood cells, plus thousands of white cells, platelets and other components.

Your skeleton is a talented fellow. His strong bone structure supports your weight, allows you to move here and there, protects your vital organs such as the brain from trauma and even manufactures blood cells in his bone marrow. A multi-tasked fellow indeed! Bone is a strong living structure constantly changing to adapt to your different movements and strength requirements. For example individuals who lift weights or do heavy labor will have larger bones than those in sedentary lifestyles. Worn-out bone is dissolved by osteoclasts (bone destroying cells); new bone is created by osteoblasts. When a bone requires more strength due to a change in physical activity, its structure will expand to accommodate the new action. For example, a tennis player's racquet arm is larger than his other arm because of ongoing adaptation.

Let's check in on activities in your digestive system, a twenty-six foot passageway from beginning to end. You open your mouth and pop in a portion of your favorite food. It begins to dissolve by chewing and by various digestive juices secreted in your mouth, stomach, small and large intestines. Wave-like peristaltic action moves the gradually disintegrating morsel along this step-by-step process. Carbohydrates are absorbed in one area, proteins and fats in other areas. Lymphatic and blood channels absorb nutritive ingredients transporting them to receiving stations in organs where they are processed and distributed to our tissues. It's all in the interest of good function, called health.

The nervous system is a vast network of sensitive neuron cells connected by tiny nerve filaments. In each moment billions of bio-electric impulses pass over these nerves conveying information from body stations to brain centers and back at tremendous speeds. You'll know it if you touch a hot stove; instant reflex action removes your hand even before the "hot" message gets to the brain. The nervous system and endocrine glands are often called the neuro-endocrine complex to indicate the close working relationship between nerve function and hormonal action. Hormones are power potions secreted by endocrine glands and discharged directly into the blood circulation network. At the rapid speed of circulation these hormones are instantly recognized throughout the body. You know how quickly a hormone like adrenaline triggers a "flight-fight" mechanism in the body when external danger threatens. The whole body goes on alert, powered-up and ready for action, and before you know it your muscles tremble. You're on guard!

Some hormones produce effects opposite to each other. Insulin from the pancreas transforms blood sugar (glucose) into glycogen, a reserve fuel to be stored in the muscles and organs. The opposite action occurs when adrenaline from the adrenal glands converts glycogen into blood sugar when called for by body activity. Here's a possibility for battle since opposites can pull and tug against each other. A similar potential war exists between the triceps and biceps muscle groups of the upper arm. In a state of contention, these two opposing forces could generate enough power to fracture the arm's humerus bone. But the wisdom of the body, that all-knowing Genie, opts instead for coordination and balance.

The body's *knight protector* is the immune system composed of nerve, endocrine and blood vascular systems. It's your watchdog, ever alert to tackle, neutralize and destroy any element from outside or from within the body which threatens to throw off precise chemical and physical balances. The immune system will also establish immunity from dangerous invasive microorganisms. A design inherent in all human biology is responsible for coordinating the thousands of interactions occurring every second. We take this for granted until normal smooth function is upset producing symptoms telling us that something is wrong.

Allopathic medicine using pharmaceutical medications attempts to balance our intricate and massive chemical mechanisms, which for whatever reason lose their equilibrium and produce unwanted symptoms. Motivated by the inconvenience of pain, we are programmed to expect instant relief from pills and potions in the pharmacy drug chest. But we don't give thought to what threw the system out of balance in the first place. What upset the Genie's balancing act and what can we do to regain our internal harmony and balance? Contrary to usual belief, good health is not a symptom-free condition but a state of endless internal shifts, changes and adaptations in the interest of maintaining balance. The Genie is our personal "Mission Control". It coordinates trillions of cells in our vast and complex networks and systems. Our world would be free of disease, starvation and heinous wars if a comparable Genie were allowed to work in human affairs. The current discord is hardly a picture of health; it is certainly not a picture of continual harmonious interactions and adaptations between nations and its peoples.

Behind all the coordinating systems at work in our bodies is the overriding penetrating presence of the Bio-Energy Field, the medium of the Genie. Its powerful chakras directly influence all systems I've described. The Field's etheric level is closest to the physical and they function together – the hands of the Genie within the glove of the physical. The wise Genie of control and coordination performs magic in us 24 hours a day, seven days a week. This magic works in greater measure when we align ourselves with these natural processes to keep the vibratory pathways clear between our Energy Field and our whole human facility, body, mind and emotions.

The Healing Charge

My vision is to restore the health of my patients by engaging their invisible powerful Bio-Energy Fields. I coined the term Vibrational Healing in the 1990s; others have picked up this term since, some perhaps before I did. My procedure restores health by clarifying a patient's Bio-Energy Field and raising the vibrational frequency of their whole system to increase physical, mental and emotional health. In my practice I have recently substituted the word *patient* with *client*, stressing for both of us the partnership involved in healing.

Joan had recently moved to Vancouver and was suffering from stress. It was a daunting transition to start her own business after being employed by a large firm in Toronto. She was also having difficulties with her teenage son. She was exhausted, had many physical aches and pains, especially the constant pain in her strained shoulder. After a number of healing sessions to clear the stress and increase the frequency of her Energy Field, Joan's health improved dramatically.

Ronald became a beacon of light once a week for 4 months. I felt safe, protected, listened to. During his sessions I could relax and truly let go of all my cares and worries. At the end of each session, I would leave feeling deeply healed and very rested. Intuitively I knew I needed deep healing. The process took 3 months – and longer to really feel like I belonged in my skin

again. My relationship with my son improved. My stress levels
were reduced and my life in Vancouver began to take shape
and form.

Stresses of living, physical and emotional traumas and unhealthy
attitudes leave blanks or gaps in an individual's Bio-Energy Field. These
"energy lacks" can lead to joint pain, muscle spasms, chronic fatigue,
poor digestion, headaches, unclear thinking, absence of vitality – in
fact almost any condition. Left undetected and not cleared over time
these distortions in The Field lead to illness. Symptoms are signs of
reduced harmony within the body. The body's homeostasis constantly
works toward functional equilibrium of all its systems. If this process
is blocked at the Energy Field level symptoms tell us something is
interfering with this process. For example, physical trauma of a bone
fracture will disrupt the Bio-Energy Field located at the break. The
extent of Field damage will depend on the severity of the fracture
and on circumstances surrounding the accident affecting other body
parts and the person's emotions, as in shock. When the damaged
area is repaired and immobilized, bones begin to knit via a complex
and magical physiological process. However complete healing will
be delayed if the Energy Field related to the injury is not cleared and
residual shock in the whole body not released. A lengthy delay in
healing could produce more physical trouble down the road. It's
unlikely that an Energy Healer would be present at the time of a trauma
but the integrity of The Field may be restored to some degree by the
care and support of individuals schooled in first-aid, by paramedics
and doctors, and by understanding family members.

A 14 year-old girl suffered from persistent pressure in her neck,
relieved only when she repeatedly hunched her shoulders and twisted

her head and neck in a strange way. Her distraught parents were told
the girl was disturbing her teachers who complained her habitual
gyrations were distracting and unnecessary. Four years earlier the girl
had been helping guide her mother into a parking space by looking
backward out of the passenger-side window. Her elbow hit the power
window button locking her neck between window and door frame.
(Power windows today are equipped with safety stops to prevent
such accidents.) Although the severe pain subsided in time assisted
by medical and chiropractic care, she was left with constant neck
pressure. My healing work on her Energy Field lasted for an hour after
which she reported feeling dizzy. A slight dizziness persisted but
disappeared after 10 days. Said her father, "She doesn't do that strange
neck gyration anymore."

Surgery, even though necessary, not only traumatizes the site of an
operation but also disturbs the whole Energy Field. Vibrational Healing
will restore the integrity of the Field as well as mending the physical
body. Taylore, one of my clients, had major surgery but the healing
process didn't go according to plan in spite of her high expectations.
She endured three weeks of severe pain before coming to see me.

*I could sense areas where my energy was blocked versus
where it was flowing. I relaxed immediately during the
sessions, and left feeling grounded, open and rejuvenated. I
felt less pain with each treatment. In about two weeks the pain
was gone and I didn't have difficulty getting in and out of the
car. I definitely felt revitalized and had more energy. The areas
between my 2nd and 3rd chakras felt open and flowing.*

Your body is capable of healing itself from any condition! If it's
restricted physically by interference and lowered frequency in your

Field, supportive Energy vibrations passing through the hands of a healer will trigger its healing capabilities. Energy Field impediments are eliminated, vital energy is restored and you are back on the road to health. Of course other treatments may also assist in physical restoration. Resonance or compatibility between you and a practitioner is important. If a tuning fork is not vibrating, it takes only the vibration/sound of a fork of the same frequency and they begin to resonate together. Joanne a young mother required surgery following a skiing accident.

> *I had just had knee surgery -- was coming out of anesthetic and morphine and antibiotics for two days. I was devastated at the idea of surgery, having never injured myself to this degree before. Just comprehending what I was dealing with was more than I had the capacity for, even without the added confusion of drugs and surgery. Previous to Ron's visit I was extremely disoriented, feeling "scattered" and tangibly like I did not have my molecules in one place. After our session I felt much more "together" as though I could now cope with the next thing before me – the trip home from the hospital. My healing is ongoing. It is now 10 weeks past surgery. I had two other sessions with Ron during the first four weeks past surgery and after each session would describe the experience as being able to move to the next "level" of healing. Pain subsided, circulation improved, swelling reduced and an overall sense of well being ensued. Frame of mind also was uplifted considerably. My impression about what Ron does is very positive and certainly useful in situations like mine.*

A doctor's greatest attribute is still the old reliable "bedside manner" which comforts and reassures a patient. But this quality is missing in the cold aloofness of physicians who callously deliver a serious diagnosis or a prognosis of a terminal illness. Patients receiving bad news in a blunt way does little for their sense of well-being. We look to doctors for empathy and inspiration which will boost our ability to get well, or at least to offer some encouragement to help us face whatever challenges are on our horizon. Similarly, the way patients prepare themselves for a regimen of antibiotics or surgery affects the outcome. Recovery depends on three vital factors: (a) patient's optimism (b) the body's ability to successfully integrate the medical procedure (c) re-powering the body's Bio-Energy Field for swift recuperation.

Margaret in her 90s was experiencing extreme pain from both deteriorating hip joints which hindered her ability to care for herself. Doctors at first refused to undertake two operations due to her age but because of her insistence and eventually being assured of her level of health, replaced both hips in one surgery. She asked me for healing sessions to speed up her recovery during post-surgical care and through two months of rehab. She returned home capable of caring for herself, walking pain-free with the aid of a cane or walker. A number of years later she was still mobile and leading an active social life.

Complementary (non-medical) therapies are often less invasive than medications or surgery but successful treatment always depends on the therapist's skill as well as his or her attitude. Two therapists using the same treatment get different results; a therapist's empathy stimulates a patient's Energy Field leading to healing in less than the usual time. Therapeutic practices including chiropractic, massage, aromatherapy, counseling, physiotherapy, naturopathy, nutrition and dietary supplements (vitamins, minerals or herbs), to name a few, can nourish the Energy Field while caring for the body. Acupuncture penetrates the body's ultra-microscopic energy meridians to release vital energy, *chi.* This centuries-old Eastern science and art is now employed by a few Western medical doctors. Homeopathy, a European procedure, has also taken root in North America. In classical homeopathy a patient undergoes extensive analysis to zero in on a specific element to be used as a remedy. The element is diluted in fluid until not even one molecule of it can be traced. However the element's energy is still contained in solution and when ingested changes the subtle Bio-Energy Field and thus body chemistry. In aboriginal cultures, tribal shamans, medicine men and witch doctors help sick members raise and transform their Energy vibrations using potions, incantations, chanting, dancing or other powerful ritual practices.

My primary concern for a person is the quality, flow and balance of their Energy Field. Of course I'm also interested in their symptom history, how they see themselves, their life style, occupation and evidence of previous traumas. During the healing session the client is urged to settle into a relaxed breathing rhythm, listening to carefully chosen music. My hands are on or few inches above his/her body as I scan to detect imbalances, energy gaps, blockages or restrictions. During this scanning process, radiation from my hands energizes the person's Bio-Energy frequencies to clear away distortions so that healing is activated. The Energy Field of a human being contains seven major chakras – spiraling power centers transmitting information from The Field to the body. I energize each chakra in turn until they respond with a greater freedom of flow. Healing is rarely instantaneous. A session may take up to an hour before adequate changes take place; these changes will continue as they return to normal activity. They will be aware that something new is happening within them. Some Field distortions are long-standing and deep-seated requiring longer time and a series of visits to raise chakra frequencies to the point where distortions are dispelled and the body re-balanced. When their symptoms recede patients appreciate feeling increasing ease. I encourage them to note the new feeling of clarity in their body so that when they're threatened again by stress, strain or new traumas they'll recall the clarity and take advantage of my help to re-balance their Field and keep their body in top condition. A cure is only a stepping-stone along the way since healing is an ongoing journey. Healing requires constant vigilance and timely corrections to stay on course, comparable to the way we continually adjust the steering wheel to keep our car on the road. Vibrational Healing is not a cure-all although I see many conditions disappear and health restored. People who live and work in extremely stressful environments also benefit. The goal is to eliminate Field restrictions so that a person's life can be enjoyed to the fullest.

A reminder: your physical, mental and emotional capacities are integrated by your invisible Energy Field. The Field's responsibility is to maintain your continuing health and strength so that you adapt more successfully to your circumstances. Your responsibility is to lead a sensible life style to help your Energy Field help you.

Cures are Rest-Stops Along the Way
enjoy your healing journey!

There is a difference between *treating illness*, and healing. The first
is foundational to the medical system we are familiar with. We seek
treatment when we are sick; we are even willing on occasion to change
our daily practices relative to food, exercise and sleep to maintain
a symptom-free body. But who thinks of going to a physician when
they feel good to enhance their wellness? Healing acknowledges
intelligent forces operating in our bodies through our Bio-Energy Fields.
The wisdom coordinating our bodies through the Energy Field is ever
ready and able to re-balance our physical systems when they are out of
sync, bringing our sick selves back to healthy function. The chiropractic
principle as I saw it recognized an innate intelligence within each
person – an intelligence capable of healing their ills. This principle
drew me to enter that study. Gradually this healing perspective became
central in my life. After graduation my intention of giving adjustments
to patients' spinal columns was to release the physical blockages
interfering with nerve flow, not to treat their diseases but to release their
own healing powers so they would get well.

This vision of healing became a passion in my life as well as in
my practice. My wife June and I were dedicated to this path. For
example, before approaching pregnancy we studied the intricacies
of a baby's development in the womb, how a woman's body

compensates to carry and nourish a growing child to term and what muscular exercises prepare a mother for a natural birth experience. Non-medicated, non-surgically assisted childbirth was rare in the 1950s but we found an obstetrician interested in a more natural approach and a hospital that would cooperate with our wishes. Even though the births of our children were not without challenging moments, June showed considerable skill in handling the cycles of labor, often to the amazement of doctors and nurses.

Our five children would encounter usual sicknesses of the growing years. But we knew for example, that a fever was their body's way of speeding up normal internal processes to take care of whatever was making them feel unwell. Of course, minor physical injuries are expected with active children. We taught them that cuts or abrasions would heal by their body's natural functions even though a band-aid would help to keep the wound clean. They trusted our healing sessions and it was rare for us to need medical consultation for them. Yes, healing is a positive approach and reveals new ways of thinking and acting.

We humans are complex living organisms not machines. Your ideal state is one of constant balanced growth and strength, in other words physical and mental health and a sense of well-being. You may recognize your spiritual dimension too whether or not you participate in a religion or belief system. While on your life's journey you encounter difficulties, problems and stress. That's the way life is. We either tackle them head-on and feel a sense of victory or we give up and feel sorry for ourselves. The dynamic of the healing process isn't understood because it's confused with treatments and remedies promising to get us well. At best they eliminate our symptoms so that we feel better and we might keep doing the things that brought on symptoms in the first place. They do not make us healthy.

Now, let's explore healing! The symptoms you encounter on your journey will be indicators of dis-ease, meaning a lack of ease or comfort. You are being told something is out of balance. Your first impulse experiencing these advance warning signs may be to dash out the door to the pharmacy for a pill or potion that promises to magically transform your discomfort back to comfort – "Frog back to Prince". We're programmed to do this by the medical profession and by pressures of continual TV and radio commercials from pharmaceutical companies. But if a treatment, therapy or prescription merely masks symptoms without thought to what's behind the warnings we aren't doing ourselves a favor. The question seldom considered is why our intricate systems have gone askew.

A diagnosis categorizes symptoms or pathologies and assigns Latin terms so that sometimes only other health professionals can decipher them. A diagnosis can relieve fears and anxieties or even point to a cure. However, some of us will latch onto a *something*-itis, a *whatever*-osis, or a *special*-emia as though it enhances our identity and makes us feel important.

All symptoms aren't advance warning signs because some conditions progress silently while pathological roots are being established. Then symptoms may appear as red alert warnings. At an advanced stage of pathology, more heroic methods of treatment may be necessary requiring strong personal dedication to a specific regimen of surgery, medication, radiation, diet or exercise. Such a course of action may be invasive in an attempt to tackle pressing physical problems. Then it's up to the healing power of your Energy

Field to regain balance and restore the body as much as possible. Fortunately red-alert symptoms are exceptions as most of us receive ample warning if we are objectively listening to our bodies. Left unchecked, an imbalance whether structural, chemical or neurological will eventually progress into a pathological condition, treatable or not.

The Human Energy Field is the first avenue of healing. A vibrational healer works directly with Field distortions to initiate healing but a physician who welcomes and reassures you, listens quietly to your situation and writes you a prescription may also affect The Field positively. *Take this pill and call me in the morning* often works. Distressing symptoms in a child often ease once the doctor speaks to frantic parents over the telephone. Many therapies can spark changes in an Energy Field – with a Vibrational Healer, an understanding counselor, nutritional guidance, physical manipulation, medication, a homeopathic remedy, surgery, etc. The placebo effect, often referred to negatively in the field of science, is actually the gift of having your sense of optimism touched, opening your Field to change. Whatever the treatment, a sense of partnership between you and a health practitioner is a winning combination – a liaison that stimulates your Energy Field. True healing involves raising your vibratory frequency to clarify Energy Field distortions, releasing your healing power. You feel the difference even before symptoms change.

During the next stage of healing, Energy Field dynamic begins to correct the physical/chemical imbalances which caused your symptoms. Your body hungers to respond to treatment perhaps in spite of a pessimistic attitude or the gravity of a disease. Ultimate success depends on your body's ability to incorporate any corrective procedure, repair the trauma and re-establish chemical and physical balances. Fortunately your internal homeostasis works constantly to balance all parts of your body. If physical deterioration is caught in time a cure is enjoyed. It may even be a miraculous cure but it's by no means the end of healing. Call it a rest-stop along the way of your journey.

As we go through life we experience many shifts and changes, external and internal, which may produce periods of discomfort. We all have the neurotic tendency to jump to conclusions that something is wrong which can propel temporary malfunction into something more serious. Don't panic! Stop and think! Often a feverish flu, a cold, excessive tiredness or depression are caused by over-fatigue, job frustration, pressures in a relationship or any form of unresolved stress. A symptom is a call for time-out. Back off! Get needed rest and relaxation and allow your body to restore itself. Make the pit stop and get back on track stronger than before. In short, listen to what your body tells you. Ask yourself: "What's this troublesome symptom really telling me? What lesson can I learn from it so I don't get strung-out and vulnerable again?"

Parents may notice that childhood and adolescent illnesses are actually part of growth cycles, physically and psychologically. If secure, because of genuine parental interest, young people emerge on the other side of these periods having grown in any number of ways. For instance you may notice that "junior" has grown an inch or two through a bout of illness. A teen crisis can be melodramatic – earth shattering to the teen, disturbing to observing adults. Parental reaction or panic can set the stage for more serious health or social problems. Cycles of change and development are normal during childhood, pre-puberty and adolescence. Similarly as adults we are wise to parent our own minds and emotions with a healing perspective and take positive action when cycles of stress and anxiety produce uncomfortable symptoms.

The medical establishment and pharmaceutical advertising would have us fighting each cycle of growth and change with medications. Don't give in to their hype. Keep in close contact with a practitioner who supports your growing understanding of how your body works and as your partner-in-healing gives invaluable assistance. Learn to enjoy your healing journey to the fullest! It's the quality of the journey that matters rather than the destination.

Healing Experiences

It is an adventure to provide alternative treatments to patients in hospitals. Years ago medical protocol was so restrictive I felt like an undercover agent even though I was there to help a patient as chiropractor or later as a vibrational healer. Nurses were uncomfortable if it was obvious I was treating the patient; doctors were usually vocal in their disagreement. Consider the situation in 1957 when our two-day old son was transferred to a children's hospital away from his mother because of temporary symptoms which might indicate a life-threatening condition in a newborn. I agreed to the transfer respecting their concern but couldn't understand why I wasn't allowed in the room with my son, let alone hold him. Nor did I get any information from a nurse or attending pediatrician as to how he was doing. However the symptoms cleared and we took baby home three days later; he hasn't been a hospital patient since. Hospitals today are generally more relaxed and welcoming of alternative healing practices. The reason is due in part to *therapeutic touch*, an energy healing by hand introduced in the 1970s to the nursing profession by Dora Kunz and Dolores Krieger.

My practice is threefold. I see clients in my office and where necessary treat them in hospitals or in their homes. Following are a few examples from my practice:

A school principal in south-eastern British Columbia found herself battling leukemia. While undergoing chemotherapy in a large Vancouver hospital she requested my care. She was isolated in her room because of lowered immune function but advised the nursing staff that I would arrive to give her vibrational healing. I was surprised no nurse came in during our session considering her condition and the elaborate intravenous equipment to which she was connected. On leaving I discovered why. A sign put on the door proclaimed: DO NOT DISTURB – ENERGY HEALING IN PROCESS. Quite an about-face from previous years to feel welcomed and respected for what I had to offer. She recovered from her illness due to her strong intention to heal, all the expert care she received and her body's ability to recuperate from a serious, often terminal, condition.

One Sunday morning I was huddled behind closed hospital curtains with Ilse, our chairs facing one another between the bed and the wall. The curtains gave us some visual privacy in a room occupied by three other patients. In the midst of the healing session I noticed two fingers gently parting the curtain. The head of a smiling nurse then popped through the narrow opening.

"Do you have everything you need?" she asked kindly.

We said we did, thanking her for her interest.

"You won't be disturbed." she said smiling, and closed the curtain, her head disappearing behind it. Three days earlier Ilse's hip was replaced. Five years before surgeons had attempted to repair her broken hip with unsatisfactory results. During her subsequent visits with me her hip discomfort was always a major factor. Eventually orthopedic doctors told her hip replacement rather than repair was preferred for individuals with advanced osteoarthritis. Before surgery she set up a number of hospital healing appointments with me in the interest of quicker recuperation. During our first session, the day after surgery, her pain was minimized by a self-controlled morphine drip. On my second visit she was seated in a chair free of intravenous connection and in relative comfort except when she shifted position. During the vibrational healing treatment we were aware of the many sounds in a hospital within and beyond the room. Then we heard the surgeon's voice as he checked on his other patients in the room. Arriving at Ilse's bed we invited him to join us in our curtained enclosure. At that time my hands were strategically placed a few inches above her body at the site of her surgery. Ilse introduced me to the young doctor and told him she was receiving a healing session. He shook my hand, smiled his approval, checked what he had to do with her and continued on his rounds. I continued healing sessions with Ilse over the next few weeks during her rehabilitation in hospital. When she returned home there was considerable improvement in her movement and subsequently she reported greater ease and mobility.

As a teenager working in his father's sawmill, Sy's powerful twist-and-push movement resulted in a back injury. Since then he has experienced periodic bouts of immobilizing pain. As a business executive in one of these painful attacks he made an appointment to see me for Vibrational Healing.

I arrived at your office after several days of pain. I could hardly get out of bed and could not get up from my knees because of pain and weakness in my muscles. During your first treatment I had moments of sharp pain even though your touch was very light, and I could barely get off your table when it was finished.

*The pain of walking was still excruciating but after an hour I
began to notice a change. A sensation of pressure I had never
felt before came across the top of my hips. The pain subsided
and I no longer felt stiff and unable to straighten up. As I
continued my appointments with you I began to feel like a new
man and I was able to go about my business.*

These days his rare twinges of pain or stiffness are usually due to an
over-exuberant golf swing. A healing session with me re-balances his
body.

Mary was experiencing back, chest, throat and sinus difficulties
when she came to my office. She admitted to a constant feeling of
anger and resentment against her boss.

*Working with anger and past hurts, I released much and felt
healed. Owning my anger was a useful step. I experienced
healing to all parts of my physical body. I was able to release
myself to the healing vibration and entered a different plane of
living. Each time there was an incredible release and healing
took place. Because of this release of tension over three years I
enjoy a happier, healthier attitude towards my work and living
in general.*

One evening many years ago when I was father of two young
children, my brother Len and his wife Irene called to say their three-
year-old son was beginning to have seizures. When I arrived at their
home Karl was cuddled on his father's lap, a perfect setting for
receiving my healing radiation after which he never experienced
another attack. Following the frightening seizure onslaught and their
release through healing, Karl announced to his parents, his younger
brother and his playmates: "Uncle Ron took the duck out of my head!"

Lydia, participating in my Vibrational Healing Workshop, was concerned about her close friend Maggie, a vibrant strong woman in her forties, a self-employed entrepreneur. She had been in hospital for two weeks with severe abdominal pain the doctors couldn't diagnose. Lydia escorted her much-weakened friend to my office during a weekend release from hospital. We helped her onto the treatment table and I asked Maggie if she was aware of any recent emotional traumas. She quickly answered, "four", before drifting off into a dream-like state. I took position at Maggie's head, Lydia at her solar plexus, as we began a healing session lasting about 90 minutes. In Maggie's own words:

A dear friend helped to carry my body to Ronald's office. My consciousness was fading rapidly; all I could hear were muffled noises from people and see faded colors around me. My friend and Ron began to give me a healing session. I felt so confused, sad and lost. In my experience it was dark as if I was in a cave. I felt like my body was full and had no room for me to come back into it. I am not sure how long I was in this process but the war began. This energy, darkness, force that was consuming my space seemed to become very powerful, I felt myself wanting to let go. Then I saw a pinhead of light. At that moment I knew I wanted so much to be in life, so much to love and share love, to live the truth of spirit given. Then the light opened up to the most amazing brilliant cross, as if it was on a hill so high, saying this light and brilliance is for all in perfect love. I went to it. As I let go to the light a sensation came over me -- a deepening of love and peace. I embraced the love with great respect and completed my union with my body.

Maggie's pain disappeared during the healing session although she remained weak. Her strength gradually returned and after 10 days she was her normal self again.

> *I have great thanks to Ron and my dear friend. Ron's work was the tool to guide me home and I am blessed for it. I now teach groups, holding a spiritual message to the opening of consciousness in the now. Thank you! In love and light.*

My practice includes patients of all ages – parents and their children and others in their eighties or nineties. Edith, a well respected retired minister and counselor called me for assistance. Later she wrote:

> *I have had chronic pain since an operation for brain tumor, which left me a "hemi-left side partial paralysis". I had less strength than needed to function well – a problem becoming more difficult since 1992 or so. Very tired, tense, and striving to continue to function. Although I cannot express the "why", I did relax with Ronald and the pain was diminished for a time after each session. The tension was relieved for a time. I still am improved but realize the problem is one which was described as chronic at the onset of my paralysis. I am older, wearing out, and have had to do less. I trust this therapist and hear recommendations from other patients as well. I am open to this therapeutic healing and have recommended it to others.*

Visiting Helen, a long-time friend in her mid-nineties is a stimulating experience because of her practical wisdom and her graceful example of living life with the end in view.

> *During and after the sessions with you I have a feeling of well being, comfort and fulfillment. Over a period of time this*

becomes a way of life. I explore new avenues and approaches and enjoy all beauty with deep appreciation. Life is a process; look always to the wider broader and expansive vision. Yield to it instead of trying to make things happen – my way. Thank you Ronald for your loving, caring and healing touch.

Although burdened with debilitating physical conditions, Margaret was able to resume her career in the high-stress movie production industry because of her association with Vibrational Healing. There were many positive improvements over five years but suddenly her breathing became so labored she had difficulty climbing the stairs to my office.

I was 48 years old when I saw my doctor for my annual check-up and she told me that my musical heart was starting to sound worse than it used to. I have had heart murmurs from a defective heart valve since birth and was told that I would need to have the valve replaced by the time I was 45. With severe difficulty in breathing a year later, I saw a cardiologist for a Stress Test but he wouldn't let me do the test because he was afraid that I wouldn't survive it. He told me he knew of people who were in better shape than I was who fell over dead. I was scheduled for an Angiogram after which I was told not to do anything but slow walking, no carrying groceries or bending over or even picking up my cat. With my surgery scheduled I saw Ron for healing sessions several times during the month of waiting.

Sher and I had become close friends while sharing in Ronald's workshop some years earlier. The bond between us prompted her to travel to Victoria to be with me every day in Intensive

*Care after the surgery, to provide healing and friendship. Then my
sister Jane, a cardiac nurse, came from Ontario and cared for me
after I got out of the hospital. I was so appreciative!*

*After the surgery the doctor told me that they couldn't figure out
how I was still alive with the hard calcified little rock that I had for
a heart valve. I didn't have opportunity to tell him of my years of
healing experience with Ron. The doctor kept pictures of my valve
to show medical students.*

*I did have trouble a few weeks later which returned me to hospital.
My heart was working so well with the new high-tech valve, my
body was being flooded with oxygen rich full volume blood flow.
My poor organs didn't know what to do with it all as they had lived
and functioned for so many years on less than 20% blood flow;
they were almost drowning now. I didn't do well in the hospital
this second time; I was dangerously over-medicated and I almost
died. I removed myself from the hospital and Ron traveled to
Victoria to share a couple of healing sessions with me. Within 24
hours I was on my way to a full and healthy recovery.*

*I had help on my journey from a number of supportive friends and
family members. I also had the fortune to understand and be able
to access the healing power of bio-energy through my years of
work with Ronald Polack. I know I would not have survived to see
my 50th birthday without him.”*

Vibrational Healing connects individuals with the ingenious powers
of their Bio-Energy Fields – their personal healing pot of gold. When
the magical recuperative influence of your Energy Field is released
within your body you are rewarded by an awareness of healing, with
increased vitality and a sense of well-being.

Distance Healing
connecting across the human energy field

There is nothing as constant in our world, indeed in our universe as we know it, as change. Life at every level is unfolding from where it is now to where it's going even in our personal lives. Conversely we tend to develop routines, habits and rigid beliefs in search of stability, and nothing threatens us as much as the suggestion of impending change – something new. For instance in the sixteenth century it was heretical and dangerous to proclaim that the world was round instead of flat. When horseless carriages appeared more than a 100 years ago they were regarded as frivolous and impractical. Even in the middle of the 20th century during the Second World War it seemed preposterous that jet-propelled aircraft would move large numbers of people around the world at breakneck speed compared to buses, trains or ships. Fifty years ago we could only imagine a man would one day walk on the moon. Could you have foreseen 25 years ago that the explosion in technology would create the vast worldwide communication of today's Internet? Before accepting new ideas we have to open our minds in the face of our insecurities. When we are wise to admit how little we know, our understanding grows. For example, how many of us realize that we each live within an invisible Energy Field, and that illness can be healed by altering the quality of that Field? Are you open to the possibility that I can heal another with a Human Energy treatment? Is it also possible to heal an individual who is 1000 miles away?

For instance, a senior woman whose husband was dying of cancer was caring for him at home. He was particularly disturbed one night and unable to settle. From their island home in the Straits of Georgia she phoned to ask if I could give him a distance healing. Later she reported:

Bob had been very restless, but he settled right down during the treatment. It was very calming to see, very peaceful. And when I have long distance healing personally it makes me feel whole. It clears my mind, makes me very peaceful.

My experience with distance healing began more than 40 years ago when, from my chiropractic office in Toronto, I connected with Roger de Winton of The Emissaries of Divine Light, living in Colorado 1500 miles away. He offered his vibrational healing support during my treatment times with more difficult cases. Suddenly these patients experienced better physical results. I was at first mystified, then beset by questions. How could this man, miles away, have a positive effect on my patients? Their conditions receded as their health improved without me changing my treatment. How did this outside force find its way through my hands and benefit those I was treating?

From Lee in Seoul, Korea following a distance healing session:

I'm feeling better but the process is very slow, considering how quickly I usually respond. I had the greatest results with your technique and am considering continuing. Here's how my progress went: I had been in pain, down my left leg, for over three months when you started treatments. I am a school teacher, and prior to hurting my leg roller-blading, I would stand to teach my classes. I had to stop standing and sit down because I was in so much pain. After only one distance treatment, I was able to stand up again to teach. As I mentioned, this was after three months of having to sit down. Also, I used to have pain in my leg whenever I walked. Since your treatments, I no longer have any pain in my leg when I walk. That has remained the case since the last healing session.

In chiropractic college I learned the principles of healing and how to use them in practice. As a clinic intern my confidence grew by witnessing the results of "before and after" spinal x-rays, blood tests and patients' symptoms. My assurance increased with the greater experience of private practice. But questions kept arising. Why didn't every patient achieve positive results even though they were open and cooperative? What was the missing ingredient? Perhaps that's what my distance-healing associate provided in those specific cases. Through a period of intense training I developed the ability to transmit healing energy to patients in my office or at a distance. The results experienced by my patients were impressive to them and to me.

When you realize that you have the power to be a healer, your ego can become inflated. So in order to remain humble I searched for answers to my own questions and those of others. What do I transmit to my patient during healing? Why doesn't it sap my energy? How does that change their physical condition? How does their immune system or other bodily rhythms function more effectively through shifts in their Energy Field? And the questions continue.

From Allana in Halifax, Nova Scotia. She was told she needed heart surgery:

December 1997: *One thing that is not a possibility – taking our time together for granted or as some kind of ritual. As I prepare to move into our session today, I know a deep sense of gratitude for you and for the opportunity that has been mine*

*for the past 7 months. During that time, my whole physical state
has changed.*

*Obviously mental and emotional have as well or the first would
not have happened. I know that I need to move into another
phase of things now. Much healing has happened. I ask myself
as we begin our time, "What am I going to do with this second
chance?"*

November 1998: *Just had to write to let you know that I have
just finished stacking ¾ of a cord of wood. My back aches,
my shoulders and arms are complaining and I haven't got even
a twinge of chest pain. I'm just dancing! If any of your clients
have any questions about the effectiveness of vibrational
healing at a distance just refer them to me! Last year at this time
I had a hard time lifting a log into the wood heater. Thank you,
my friend.*

The stage is set. At a time arranged with a patient [in this case,
Allana] I sit alone in my office. She is relaxed and quiet in a comfortable
spot at home, perhaps listening to soft music or to my CD, *A Healing
Session with Ronald.* I extend my Energy to connect with her Field
and instantly I feel her presence. This is possible because both our
Bio-Energy Fields exist within a common larger Field. I may perceive
shadows of her symptoms in my hands or my body. As the session
continues I feel changes in her Field. I begin to work toward an overall
clarity and balance in her Field. I direct my attention to the specific
physical and emotional areas affected by each chakra as I would if she
were in my office. As I perceive a disturbed area in the patient coming
clear I move onto the next chakra until I feel clarity in her whole Field.
By the time 20 or 30 minutes have passed my sensing of her symptoms

has changed. I may feel a symptom increase as the body makes corrections, or they will recede immediately. My Field sparks changes in her Bio-Energy Field so that healing can begin. The few testimonials I've included in this chapter illustrate successful distance healings of my patients.

From Valerie in Kincardine, Ontario:

A distance healing with Ronald is as powerful for me as a healing in his office. With anticipation I receive his healing energy and love as we move through my chakras together. I feel relaxed, rejuvenated and reborn. Sometimes all I have to do is think about Ronald and I receive his healing energy. Thank you Ronald.

I keep current with latest scientific developments relating to my passion for normal and abnormal physiology, practical psychology and healing human ills. My vision is to create Bio-Energetic sessions transforming disease into health; they are also significant investments in health maintenance. Incidentally the horrendous costs of health care would be reduced if individuals took responsibility for their health before sickness strikes. Waiting until we are sick before seeking professional assistance is a flaw in our society and in our personal programming. What are we doing to maintain the level of health that we have and prevent diseases from setting in? Why not become familiar with a natural approach that constantly stimulates our bodies to heal themselves? Vibrational Healing has a significant part to play in this new perspective.

Much medical-related science focuses on microscopic bacteria and viruses, based on the theory that disease comes from outside of us and must be attacked with external agents or drugs. Medical doctors and scientists depend heavily on the pharmaceutical products to develop medications to treat illnesses, while at the same time enriching the industry's shareholders. On the other hand, pioneers in quantum science and the new physics continue researching vibrational frequencies of the human dynamic in the interest of improving the human condition and the ecology of the Earth.

One such pioneer is Dr. Valerie Hunt, author of *Infinite Mind: Science of the Human Vibrations of Consciousness*. She had specialized in traditional psychology and physiology but changed direction 25 years earlier. She experimented with high-frequency instruments to measure human vibrations and to clinically investigate mystical levels of emotional states. Dr. Hunt was probably the first scientist to detect the vibrations of pain, disease and illness, in addition to vibrations of emotional and spiritual states.

From June S. in Victoria:

I lay down on my bed as you suggested. I really didn't know whether or not I "believed" it would work but knew that at the very least, I'm away from my computer and resting on my bed. Well, within moments I actually had the same responses I had when I was on the table in your office. I couldn't believe it. My body seemed to melt down releasing toxins and within about 10 minutes I was fast asleep. When I woke, I felt refreshed and out of pain.

In *The Field: The Quest for the Secret Force of the Universe*, American investigative journalist Lynne McTaggart documents experiments of researchers working in physics and the human field. In the chapter, *The Healing Field*, she reports on scientific studies to answer these questions:

How powerful was intention as a force and exactly how infectious
was the coherence of individual consciousness? Could we actually
tap into the "field" to control our own health or even to heal others?
Could it cure really serious diseases like cancer? Was the coherence
of human consciousness responsible for psychoneuroimmunology,
the healing effect of the mind on the body? If non-local effects
could be marshalled to heal someone, then a discipline like distant
healing ought to work.

She documented controlled double-blind research studies in
remote/distance healing employing a number of healing practitioners.
Each one used a different healing technique. The result was
considerable improvement in cardiac patients and AIDS victims. She
said, "It didn't seem to matter what method you used, so long you held
an intention for a patient to heal."

From Eleanor in Lakefield, Ontario:

Over the past year I have had great discomfort from left
shoulder and arm, left hip and leg, to the extent it inhibited
sleeping and everyday movements. With the blessing of weekly
healing sessions with Ronald, I have been able to slowly
learn to relax body, mind and spirit and flow with the warm
and often tingling sensation of healing. Thus, today I have no
discomfort with the exception of some in the left upper arm
occasionally. Following a session I usually sense a greater inner
calm as though I can handle whatever might beset me. I am
thankful for Ronald's gift from the Universal Source that is able
to touch in with my Life Source.

Our personal Bio-Energy Field is connected to the Fields of
others, thus opening the possibility for distance healing. The healing

current in my experience transcends distance instantaneously to spark regeneration within the receiver. This is especially evident if the patient is aware of the process and shares the healing intention. Distance is not a barrier!

Is Dying Also Natural?
meeting our greatest fear

We're all born with a fear of dying. Perhaps it's part of a universal urge to self-preservation thought common to all species. But some animals sensing the end is near retreat to a quiet place and without fuss or fanfare give up the ghost. As humans we know we are not going to live forever even though we're unlikely to talk easily about our demise or that of a friend sitting next to us. We repel from the thought of death and especially the act of dying. These are feelings we have in common with everyone.

When someone close dies it is natural and healthy to grieve our loss; a deeply personal matter whether we show it outwardly or not. I've often thought that expressing my grief over a departed friend or loved one may be a heart-felt bon voyage and support of them as they find their way in a new non-earthly cycle. But how much of our emotional pain is about losing them and how much is anxiety about our own mortality **– the great mystery of life and death as it relates to "me" – when, where, how, etc.?** I suspect we share that with almost everyone but it's not a popular topic of conversation.

In general we may discuss theories about "after-death" but do we consider where we were before conception? Perhaps we return there naturally – a place difficult to imagine? Maybe you've given it some thought? There are as many ideas about life after death as there are people, related to religious promises, philosophical concepts or intuitive sensitivity. The clergy's intention is to comfort us while urging us to conform to the "good life" on earth, insuring preferred choice of destination afterward. A comforting thought perhaps?

Dying is as much a part of living as living is a part of dying. We're all destined to die even though we act like we'll live forever – unconscious denial. However, as long as we ignore the inevitable we are missing a key to the magic of living. In *Tuesdays With Morrie* by Mitch Albom, terminally ill Morrie Schwartz said, "The truth is, Mitch, once you learn how to die, you learn how to live." That's a provoking statement, is it not? What's missing in death denial is a perspective of what our earth journey is all about. How can we live confidently if we're living our lives under a pall of fear, usually looking for a great mama, papa or a shining savior to console us and "make it all better"? Dying is the natural finale to our time on earth. Much suffering in dying, as in living, results from not being conscious of the struggles inside us; current ones that are festering or issues from long ago we have forgotten but never resolved. To uncover these hidden conflicts and begin dealing with them is to move toward greater ease in living; the same ongoing process prepares us for a more comfortable and peaceful release. There is a process to dying similar to the ongoing growth and adaptation in living, which we might call healing.

David Kuhl wrote a book *What Dying People Want*:

For more than fifteen years I have worked, as a doctor, with people who were dying. They taught me many things – for example, that I didn't know how to talk to them about dying. And peculiar as it may seem, they taught me a lot about living. People who are dying are still living. Living, like dying, includes choice.

*My grandfather spent the last days of his life in an extended
care facility. It was there that he said, "Dying is hard work – not
the physical part, but that part which is the inside of me, the
work about who I am, who I have been, and who I will be.*

Dr. Kuhl found significant suffering of patients in palliative
care related to unresolved issues they were carrying, knowingly or
unknowingly. Hospices are known for their peaceful atmosphere. In
the surround of caregivers, loving family and doctors finding effective
medication for any physical pain there was something missing. Who
was with them, not denying the upcoming death but encouraging
them, asking questions and listening so they could share their anxieties
and tell their stories? Our stories whether we're living or dying are often
a surprise to us as they come to light. (Living or dying – is there really a
difference? The dying are living too.)

One of the greatest gifts anyone can find is a *listener*: someone
who is attentive to receive what we have to say, who is not going to
judge us, give advice or counter our story with their own experiences.
Listeners in this sense are few and far between even among
professionals who we might suppose are trained and willing to see us
for who we are, willing to hear what we have to say without judgment
and not feel compelled to correct our thoughts or tell us "what we
should do".

A person in transition likely has emotional things close to the
surface. I was visiting my father in his 94th year some months before his
death and he began to tell me, in tears, how deeply hurt he was that
his mother never accepted him at his birth or anytime later. He felt it
was because he was born with a hair lip and cleft palate. As he spoke

with me he was not concerned about the physical condition, requiring surgery when he was very small, but was still deeply hurt with her non-acceptance of him compared to his brothers, as he experienced it. It didn't matter what the facts were over ninety years earlier; it was his feeling of being abandoned that was still with him. I was touched by his openness with me and I trust I conveyed my understanding of how he felt. When he was in a care facility later his wife, my mother, visited him every day. But he was troubled about their physical separation and his anxiety came out in sarcastic comments to her that she was carrying on with another man. Abandonment again! It was disturbing for her to handle this accusation and difficult to have an open conversation with him because of a lack of privacy. Eventually a nurse sensed this and provided a room where they could visit alone for as long as they wanted. My mother shared with me that they had a very straightforward conversation about the preciousness of their seventy years of marriage, their fine children, grandchildren and great grandchildren and she assured him she had never been interested in another man. She told me they re-connected in love. Within a couple of days he died peacefully in his sleep and although she deeply missed him, she was relieved that all was clear between them.

My sister and I have always been close. Her husband, having only months to live, expressed his concern to me about leaving my sister on her own. I was direct with him, "Richard, since you and Eleanor became a couple 40 years ago I've never had a worry about her because I knew she was with the right man. You cared for her and looked after her so well. Thank you Richard! I know she will be fine after your departure." He was relieved to hear my words. He passed away quietly a few months later, at home with his wife and his best male friend at his side. My sister has done well facing the challenge of being alone for the first time in her life, re-creating herself as a single woman, enjoying new adventures while still missing her closest friend.

My brother Len had been suffering from lymphatic cancer for a few years without success and his doctors suggested a final regimen of chemotherapy to try to turn the disease around. I was visiting with him in the cancer clinic after two weeks of constant chemotherapy when the doctor arrived and announced, "Mr. Polack, I'm sorry to tell you there isn't any change in your condition and we don't have any other options for you." His wife and three teen-age sons lived 300 miles away and it was just before Christmas. I pulled some strings to arrange a flight home the next day – this would be his last flight; he was returning home with a few months to live facing unknown discomforts of a cancer death. When I visited him the next day he was up and dressed, ready to go to the airport. As we sat on the bed chatting while I rubbed his back, I suggested a healing session and he was keen that we do that. He was so relaxed during the healing when I said to him softly, "Len, you just need to let go and let this cycle work out", thinking of his challenge of going home to die. He mumbled something to me which I didn't understand but I felt he was agreeing with what I said – and then lapsed into a coma which he never came out of. He died about eight hours later. As shocking as that was for me, our family, especially his wife and sons and our parents, we all honored the choice of peaceful departure as his final experience. I miss my brother but I wouldn't miss him any less if he had experienced a drawn-out uncomfortable demise.

We create masks when we are very young as we stretch to adapt to domestic and sibling surrounds, to survive early challenges and protect our innocent hearts. We forget how vulnerable we felt as a child trying to live up to people's expectations and be loved by those we looked up to, whether or not we had "perfect" or "good-enough" parents. The mask is the persona we each developed and still carry unknowingly. It determines how we present ourselves to others, as a friend, lover, husband or wife, business associate, mother, father, etc. – all the roles we play in life. Reason was not involved in creating the mask; it was a necessity of the moment for the child, a matter of survival in a world we didn't understand. We never remember as a child, teen or adult that we even wear a mask let alone why we crafted it as we did. We think our persona is who we are. But as we tell our personal story or any part of it, difficult or wonderful, we speak from the essence of who we are, the one behind the mask. Our real self telling the story begins to have new insights about our journey; things begin to make sense, fall into place, and over time we begin to feel better about ourselves. This is not a simple process. It requires confidence and trust between listener and storyteller and likely will not unfold all at once. Personal storytelling can also be done by oneself through journaling. Just begin by writing down what you are feeling and see what reveals itself as you continue to write. Our story comes out at times in bits and pieces like a jig-saw puzzle, each experience part of a larger picture revealing deeply held feelings that have been supporting the mask and hiding one's true nature, one's innate quality of soul. Telling one's story to oneself or someone you trust is a healing process that brings renewed confidence in living. And it can bring a living person, who is dying, ease and relaxation to move into the final earthly release.

The privilege of being with a loved one who is dying can be a powerful and intimate experience. You may have touched that poignant energy listening to someone at a funeral or memorial service recalling close and meaningful moments before the death of the recently deceased. Often it's awkward visiting a dying person because we are so uncomfortable with thoughts of their upcoming departure, and our own mortality. We might try to convince the person that they will get well or direct conversation to the weather, Aunt Fanny's hat or some other convenient distraction. It's a delicate matter for sure and a challenge to be as natural as possible. Of course we'd be ill advised to impose a callous announcement of the coming event. And yet being quietly sensitively present you may perceive an opportunity to encourage them to share with you what is really on their mind even though they may not be aware of their feelings until you gently ask. It's helpful to express love and appreciation for the value you place on your relationship with them. You could remind them of how they have affected your life positively and offer specific examples about how they have lived their life and what they have accomplished. This would help remind a person how valuable their life has been – an encouraging boost to their sense of meaning in the face of their present uncertainty. It may also prompt them to share some of their deeper thoughts with you. If you have seriously considered your own life journey and its eventual end, you will find more ease in moments with a friend or loved one and be aware what you might say to assist them approaching their earthly finale. For most people there is value in being physically touched at a time like this; something as simple as your hand in theirs, touching their arm or sitting close to them. Death is inevitable – not contagious. Let's enhance the natural process of death with closeness and genuine friendship. What a person may be suffering physically is less important to them than their longing for comradeship and encouragement. If you find yourself geographically distant from a person you care for who may be approaching their end, writing to them about your feelings for them can be a special gift whether they are able to read themselves or have someone read your words to them.

There is only one way to come into this world. There are many ways to die. However the end comes -- unexpectedly, violently in an accident or a gradual process, birth and death are natural bookends of a lifetime on earth. I have witnessed the hard work and unbelievable joy in the natural experience of a woman giving birth, largely because she had tempered her fear with common sense and deliberate preparation, physically and mentally. We would be equally wise in facing our fear of death starting now, whatever our age. There is much beauty missed in life and death because we're so bound with unresolved emotional issues that could be released through personal introspection, reviewing our life events and sharing some of our stories and concerns with an understanding friend or professional counsel. We can assist others in the process if we accept the challenge of approaching our own demise in a more natural way!

Social Survival

Your human organism is both physical and non-physical. Your body is your instrument of interaction with people and other life forms – your means of contributing to this world through your thoughts, words and actions. As you become more perceptive of your personal Energy Field your sense of self expands and your view of health is no longer limited to the physical body. Your invisible Field needs as much care as your physical body if you are to stay healthy. This book opens doors to new understanding and stimulates you to adopt new attitudes and ways of thinking.

Traumas and shocks, physical or emotional, are part of our life experience. But rather than playing the victim, complaining about the results of our traumas we can heal and grow by caring for body, mind and emotions through our personal Energy Field, i.e. taking personal responsibiltiy. The Field is a powerful reservoir for healing but is vulnerable to negative intrusions as are our bodies and our feelings. Damage at the Field level if ignored will reflect itself in illness sooner or later. Through Vibrational Healing we can take personal responsibility for our health at all levels.

Stress is synonymous with living or are you able to avoid it? Its effect on us may be alleviated if we learn skills to handle challenging circumstances. Even low-level stress over time will undermine our health; it creeps up gradually and takes us unaware. High stress levels increase our need for Vibrational Healing to re-balance body and mind through our personal Energy Field. Otherwise the poison from accumulated emotional and physical stress will take its toll.

Our world is becoming an increasingly complex and invasive place to live in. Before technology took hold, people lived more locally primarily aware of activities in their own communities. Not anymore. No matter where you live today you are constantly bombarded with information from around the world. The news media delights to bring you sensational reports of disasters, wars, famine and latest diseases to threaten you or terrorists to do you in. Security is escalating to such an extent that we begin to feel like prisoners in our own countries. Talk about stress! So called "health news" can scare us half to death based as it often is on assumptions and speculations from incomplete polls and research. The opinions widely broadcasted lead directly into pharmaceutical advertising, subtly increasing our fear and anxiety levels. These insidious forms of stress suppress our immune system and drain our vitality; we begin to lose our natural vibrancy to cope with daily circumstances. As a result the healing potential of our body is sabotaged.

In an e.mail conversation with Dr. Grant Johnson, a veteran psychologist living in Arizona, I asked for his thoughts on increasing stress and anxiety.

He wrote in reply:

There is no question that the increase of stress has been monumental and is an ongoing threat to our immune systems. Many family doctors will tell you that stress is the biggest cause of the physical symptoms presented by their patients. Today, depression is the number one illness in the U.S. Despite a proliferation of prescription drugs, these conditions persist and they are no doubt having a profound effect upon individual health. Anxiety symptoms are legion such as panic attacks, exaggerated startle-response, hyper-vigilance, free-floating anxiety and the list goes on. If not mitigated, these symptoms lead to depression and physical breakdown.

Does Dr. Johnson have suggestions to counteract this form of disease?

Yes, get help from someone who can reach these subconscious levels of anxiety. This could very well include departures from Western Medicine, utilizing proven alternative approaches designed to decrease anxiety and release stress, improving our overall health.

How do we insure our personal well-being surrounded as we are with fear, anxiety and depression whether or not we're aware of it? How do we protect and enhance the magical healing processes constantly working in us, bio-energetically and physically? Here are some ideas:

- Exercise and relax in Nature – enjoy the beauty and smell the flowers, embrace a tree, inhale seaside aromas, marvel at the mountains, play with your children, grandchildren and the pets. They'll invigorate you, especially when they are appreciated.
- Choose entertainment that inspires or makes you laugh – check the quality of TV shows or movies you watch including the commercials; after all you are either positively affected or negatively infected by what you watch and listen to.
- Monitor the time you spend on the news – it has a negative

influence on us. By all means keep in touch but don't wallow in it and don't go to bed on it.

- Changes in routine are refreshing – remember spontaneity!
- Tell someone you appreciate them – and why.
- Laughter is good medicine. So are understanding friends.
- Quiet meditation and inner listening give you valuable direction.
- Professional counsel will help you see what you're missing.
- Vibrational Healing clears the effects of stress and frees your healing energy.

You have the option for greater enjoyment by transforming negative situations into positive ones. But it won't just happen! We are all challenged to master skills of living healthy, meaningful lives. Learn to access the rainbow of your Bio-Energy Field and its healing pot of gold. Vibrational vitality is yours to discover and enjoy.

Part Two:

Dynamics of Mind and Heart

Your Attitude

It's one of those days!

Joe stubs his toe getting out of bed. He cuts himself shaving. His toast is burned and his eggs overcooked. People cut him off in traffic and he gets caught in the the slow lane driving to work. The elevator is crowded with people who jostle him getting on and off. Things continue to go downhill through his working day. He might relieve the pressure by going for a drink after work, maybe with that attractive woman on Reception? In any case when he gets home he barks at his wife and yells at the kids; why can't they understand what a miserable day he's had? There is tension at the dinner table and he later falls asleep in his living room chair exhausted.

That stubbed toe seemed to set the pace for his entire day. But was it the pain in the toe or did that trigger the memory of a trauma he had been carrying inside for some time?

Could he have broken the downward spiral of the experience of being a victim by taking a few thoughtful breaths to change his attitude – about the toe, the traffic, a teenage wound from his father, or an unrequited love affair from his 20's? Is it possible to recognize and change his own attitude or should he seek professional help? Could such a change affect his daily experiences at home and at work, maybe for the rest of his life?

No matter what I do!

Maryelle projects a positive attitude, longing to be respected by her associates, trying to be successful in business, hoping to develop and hold a close relationship. She discovers no matter how hard she tries, nothing works out the way she wants it. Have previous traumatic experiences she doesn't remember infected her Field? Have these traumas resulted in persistent distortions within her make-up sabotaging her best intentions? Smiling on the outside, seething on the inside. Do you know anyone like that? She may need expert help to expose that hidden trauma.

A persistent shadow!

Jane was a bright young woman with a sound family background. After she found a good job she complained about her Company – about what's wrong with the government – about how badly employees and customers were being treated. Now as a single parent in her late forties with three children she is on welfare. She knows all the angles. She hasn't held a job for over twenty years. What is it in her Field, harbored in her subconscious, that casts a shadow on her life? She is one of many who try hard to be successful but seem thwarted from a deeper level; they feel the world owes them a living. Yet I know single mothers and couples who struggle financially but express attitudes that influence their careers and their children in positive ways.

These examples show that whether or not we are aware of our attitudes, or what's behind them historically, they do have a determining effect on our present experiences. Consider a ship's engines that move the vessel through the water while its destination is determined by how the helmsman positions the rudder. You are the helmsman by the quality of your attitude, your rudder. What are your attitudes really, toward: your job, your spouse, your friends, your country, your abode, your car – most important, how do you feel about you? You can easily give a surface answer to these questions but your reactions may be hidden, locked in your Energy Field. Unfortunately we are unaware of the activity within our Field, except when it reaches our conscious mind. We may suspect though that persistent physical and psychological symptoms, or repetitive failures that plague us, may be due to long-standing distortions in our Field. It's known that muscles and other tissues in our bodies retain memories of past traumas long after we've forgotten them. These memories of past pain may be the rudder directing our experiences now.

Denial of our deeper emotions gives us license to blame someone else for what we feel and for our shortcomings. This defensiveness is common in our culture and seems an easier way to deal with pressure in the short term. To accept responsibility involves examining our feelings to see how they are pushing our experience in a certain direction. A wise friend once said to me: "If you don't change the direction in which you are going, you'll end up where you're headed."

For a number of years I participated in a non-profit organization that held a vision to lift human consciousness to a creative level where peace and harmony would prevail. I became a leader, counselor, healer and teacher. We were admonished to always express a generative attitude, as individuals and as a group, to be a positive influence in the world. If we found ourselves in a negative frame of mind we were encouraged to *change our attitude*. It was acceptable to express qualities of optimism, humility, thankfulness, forgiveness, etc. When feeling angry or critical we would switch to a more mellow expression by repressing reactive feelings which we felt were destructive to ourselves and others. However intense repressed feelings don't go away but remain lodged in the unconscious of the Bio-Field and pop back up when we're under pressure. Who knows what damage we do to ourselves as these submerged feelings distort the free flow of our health-giving Bio-Energy. My experience of "maintaining a clear attitude" in this organization was an enjoyable way to live as long as the members were loyal to each other within the stated larger purpose – "one for all and all for one, for the good of the whole world". We accomplished magical growth in worldwide membership and in the development of exemplary performing arts. But as the network of people matured we felt compelled to shift from a patriarchal management to a more consensual democratic style. This opened Pandora's Box. Feelings, attitudes and ideas repressed for so long broke free and swamped our daily interactions, especially at painful lengthy meetings during which we attempted to sort out our differences and achieve a new style of working together. Where did our sweet, harmonious community go? When agreement was clear and coherence among us was strong we accomplished whatever we set out to do. It seemed we had a magical touch. But as we began to expose our many repressed opinions creating a lack of trust among us, even simple plans went awry.

Every group generates a positive or negative force, depending on the quality of the collective attitude. Often in sports we witness the lesser team, rated the underdog, going into a championship game coming out the winner. We might say, "They played as a team; they were really together!" The same is true in business. A company that values its employees, listens to their feedback and takes the trouble to develop team management skills, will usually outperform the competition. Referring again to the analogy of the ship at sea – it's not just a matter of the helmsman providing the right direction; the motors will also access greater power from the collective energy.

Often a person who comes to Vibrational Healing with physical symptoms will experience dramatic changes in attitude as their healing progresses -- sometimes a new lease on life. I will hear from a spouse or fellow worker, "Yes, I know his arthritis and indigestion are improving but since he's been going to see you he is a much easier man to live with." With other patients a trusting openness gradually develops where it's natural to let deeper feelings surface in conversation. Sometimes as patients become aware of their hidden attitudes, distortions in their Fields automatically begin to defuse and negative effects upon their bodies and in their lives begin to dissolve. But it may be necessary to deliberately resolve to expose and change uncovered attitudes and the habits they spawn – whatever it takes to release constrictions in ones Energy Field and enjoy a new freedom of health and self-expression.

During high school I was impressed with the *Power Of Positive Thinking* by Norman Vincent Peale. I discovered that if I was optimistic at the outset I could control the outcome of certain projects, activities and relationships. But there were some matters in my life where a relatively surface change in attitude didn't ensure the outcome. I have learned since that memories within my Field, of which I am not aware, may undermine my initial optimism with undesirable results. Anger, disappointment, resentment or other feelings will persist in my Field until I remember why they are there and learn how to deal with them; this could require professional assistance. While a mentor's wise guidance may be helpful it is always up to me to make the attitudinal changes to clear my Field.

Your Field contains everything you have ever experienced. Positive experiences are a good foundation for success but negative ones can stifle your expression. You may be blown about by cruel winds of circumstance or encumbered by the flotsam and jetsam of negative experiences locked in your Bio-Energy Field. But as you choose to recognize these shadows in your Field you will have greater control of attitudes that color your expression, resulting in a more positive experience. Clear attitudes open the door to your natural vitality and creativity.

The Psyche of the Human Energy Field

The vastness of our personal Energy Field puts our physical stature in perspective as the smallest part of us. We give undue importance to our physicality considering the many non-physical influences creating our physical presence, our health and our expression. We are programmed from an early age that health is constantly threatened by invasive entities from outside, like bacteria and viruses. So treatment of disease would depend on medications to attack the perpetrators, microscopic or not. This medical model is the way we think because it's been dominant in our upbringing and education supported by constant pharmaceutical advertising. But beyond that model focused on our physical dimensions are complexities of our invisible psyche influencing health and sickness. What really makes us tick? What makes us so susceptible to microorganisms and negative effects from stress? Why do we express ourselves the way we do and how does that affect physical health, mental/emotional well-being and quality of expression?

Psyche has a broad definition: human soul, spirit or mind; the mental or psychological structure of a person. The psyche within your Energy Field shapes your personality. 20th century psychiatrists Freud, Jung, Adler and others probed deeply to understand invisible factors that determine our behavior. Dr. Jung talked about the collective unconscious, a sea of energy enveloping all of us composed of human behavior patterns, some imprinting on us individually. He named combinations of these behavior patterns complexes – present in us even though we're not conscious of them.

Complex – defined in psychoanalysis: a group of ideas with strong emotional tone which have been transferred by the conscious mind (and collective unconscious – Jung) into the unconscious and from there influence the personality.

Common usage of the word, *complex*, comes out in: anxiety complex, oedipus complex, persecution complex, inferiority complex, etc.

The influence of complexes on our expression may be creative, inventive, inspiring, depressing, violent, moody, etc. Whether generative or destructive these invisible complexes out of our own subconscious as well as out of the collective unconscious author our feelings, shape our thoughts and find expression through our words and actions. This unconscious imprinting, modified by individual genetic and hereditary influences reflect in our expression. Do we really have freedom of choice in what we say and do? One person is inherently afraid of heights; another thrives in high places like ironworkers constructing skyscrapers, trapeze artists in the circus and skydivers who jump for the thrill. You may be afraid of water while someone else is drawn to it – a diver, a surfer or long-distance swimmer. For no apparent reason you may be wary of men with beards or women wearing kerchiefs on their heads; another person may be attracted to these same people. Some complexes seem to be more instinctual like the fear of falling or the urge to self-preservation. Our unconscious gathers other factors from experiences before birth and during childhood because of our interactions with parents, siblings, teachers and others in authority who leave an impression on us. The surprising intensity of an instantaneous feeling reaction you have today about a person or circumstance will show how deeply you are affected and how dominant that particular complex is in your make-up.

"I didn't know I had such deep feelings about that situation but when I look at it now my reaction was quite illogical."

"When someone does that, I take it personally and it always upsets me!"

"I've always been afraid of heights." Why?

There are many complexes within your unconscious program, on default as it were, whether you express them outwardly or hold them internally. These patterns determine attitudes, shape intention, color what happens in our experience, our sense of well-being and even our tendency to be well or sick. Not realizing how pervasive these complexes are in what we say and do, we blame others for what we feel, resent our circumstances and even project our fear and anger on a deity. We might say,

"That person always brings this up in me – I feel it the moment I see him or her."

or "Under that kind of pressure, I couldn't have done otherwise."

maybe "I was inspired by God."

– or the reverse "The Devil made me do it."

or "I am being punished; it's my karma."

If we are aware, as Pogo said, "We have found the enemy and it is us!" we will awaken to see events and people in a more objective light rather than blaming someone else for what we are feeling in a moment. *You are awakening your choices by reading this chapter.* Walking into a room full of strangers you will now be aware that snap judgments of them are probably not based in fact but are reflections of your complexes. Then you can soften or actually change your attitude; be open, understanding, more compassionate in your evaluations and how you interact with each person. If such honesty were typical (especially of individuals who form organizations, communities and nations, even the United Nations) our larger world would not be such a mess of conflict and war. Through the eyes of the media we might conclude that there is a dominance of negative, indeed sociopathic, people on earth. Is that an accurate assumption or is it based on repetitive emphasis and sensationalism of reporters and news editors? Do we have any idea how these assumptions impact our expression and overall well-being? Even before exposure from media each of us acquired a variety of complexes, both positive and negative. Some complexes bring out our finer qualities: hidden talents, intuition, creative capabilities and keen perceptions. These positive attributes are gifts that mold a substantial personality, an ability to cope successfully within a variety of social and domestic circumstances bringing a cohesive influence into our surround.

At a deep primal level, hard-wiring common to all people are bedrock structures called archetypes. *Archetype* meaning *first form*. Jung suggested these are equivalent to the instincts of animals. They are present no matter what and are basic building blocks of the psyche, reflective of finest inherent qualities of being human. Some psychologists have called archetypal force, *libido*. Freud believed it as fundamentally sexual; Jung believed that libido is a generalized force that expresses itself through a range of impulses as well as through sexuality. The foundation of a rich fulfilling life depends on our ability to access, integrate and express the clear energy and power of our positive or primary archetypes. When we inadvertently distort these energies under pressure of our complexes, our basic archetypes will be "in shadow" and their power will wreak havoc in our lives and produce diseases in our bodies. In other words these archetypal resources are powerful, generatively or destructively, depending on clarity or shadow. You might begin to see them as members of your personal advisory board. Considering my advisory board, I might liken the "I", the one choosing my expression in each moment, as the president of the board. As I become sensitive to my archetypal board members and align with the generative support of their positive values, I develop the quality of life my personal intuition directs, the kind of life I want. As my discernment increases I recognize shadows in my board members and find ways to clear those distortions or at least avoid them in what I express. Archetypal energies are a gift but in shadow they don't serve us well or those around us. Consider this metaphor on shadows of the psyche, excerpted from American poet Robert Bly's book, *A Little Book On The Human Shadow*:

> *When we were one or two years old we had what we might visualize as a 360 degree personality. Energy radiated out from all parts of our body and all parts of our psyche. A child running is a living globe of energy. We had a ball of energy, all right; but one day we noticed that our parents didn't like certain parts of that ball. They said things like: "Can't you be still?" or "It isn't nice to try and kill your brother."* ["Don't" and "no" are two popular words in parenting.] *Behind us we have an invisible bag, and the part of us our parents' don't like, we, to keep our parents' love, put in the bag. By the time we go to school our bag is quite large. Then our teachers have their say:*

"Good children don't get angry over such little things." So we
take our anger and put it in the bag. By the time my brother and
I were twelve in Madison, Minnesota we were known as "the
nice Bly boys." Our bags were already a mile long.
Then we do a lot of bag-stuffing in high school. This time it's
no longer the evil grownups that pressure us, but people our
own age. So the student's paranoia about grownups can be
misplaced. I lied all through high school automatically to try
to be more like the basketball players. Any part of myself that
was a little slow went into the bag. My sons are going through
the process now; I watched my daughters, who were older,
experience it. I noticed with dismay how much they put into
the bag, but there was nothing their mother or I could do
about it. Often my daughters seemed to make their decisions
on the issue of fashion and collective ideas of beauty, and they
suffered as much damage from other girls as they did from
men. So I maintain that out of a round globe of energy the
twenty-year-old ends up with a slice.

In other words we make choices through our lives under pressure
of wanting to be loved by those we respect and be acceptable in
the eyes of our peers. This represses some of our powerful archetypal
energies into shadow, into the bag as Bly suggests, leaving our state
depleted and distorted. As well, shadow or imprisoned energy
comes out in our expression, outwardly destructive or internally
self-destructive. Is it any wonder why people realize such a small
percentage of their potential? We begin to see how often we are our
own worst enemy.

In relationships people mostly choose their mates by chemistry of attraction. Perhaps they touch through initial infatuation, hopefully deepening love later, a dynamic of energetic synchrony, a blend of certain archetypal qualities – a union of hearts. They commit to join together knowing the strength of their togetherness. Later, "after the honeymoon is over" pressures of close living will erupt shadows of those same powerful archetypes that drew them together and will threaten confidence in their love. "I didn't marry this person!" now looking very different as shadows emerge in their expression. "Shadow-boxing" may be an apt description of domestic disharmony. Obviously it takes good communication skills based on personal honesty to clear over-riding shadows so the underlying power of love can re-emerge even stronger because of victory over conflict. A counselor may be valuable in learning those skills.

Let's consider qualities of some archetypes. Robert Moore and Douglas Gillette described four basic archetypes in their series of books describing *King Warrior Magician Lover*. Their writing was in response to a surge of interest within the Men's Movement in the 1980s. Similar archetypes present in women can be described as Queen, Warrior, Magician, Lover. I am not suggesting that men and women are the same. Jung spoke of the foundational *anima* spirit/energy in women as different from the *animus* in men; while both are present in each – anima is dominant in women and animus in men, usually. Dr. Marianne Legato states in *Why Men Never Remember and Women Never Forget*:

> *Men and women think differently, approach problems differently, emphasize the importance of things differently and experience the world around us through entirely different filters.*

Considering the four basic archetypes King, Warrior, Magician,

Lover: The king or queen archetype possesses qualities of true authority; reasonableness, integrity and a concern for the entire kingdom of body, mind and heart. This sovereign influence stabilizes chaotic emotion and "out of control" behaviors, bringing a sense of centeredness and calm. This is the capacity to care for and bless ourselves, and others. In a personal sense how much do we know of these qualities? We may be more aware of their shadows in others rather than ourselves, like the merciless tyrant king or queen who can't tolerate criticism, or the passive sovereign hungering to be seen and respected and who is fearful and defensively hostile to others and himself.

The word "warrior" tends to be socially unpopular and might be considered not worthy of consideration as a basic archetype. No wonder! We've suffered centuries of willful destruction and cruelty inflicted mostly by sadistic male energy whether in individuals, gangs, the military (directed by political leaders), or corporations where profit-at-any-cost is primary. Less dramatic but equally as destructive as this *sadistic*

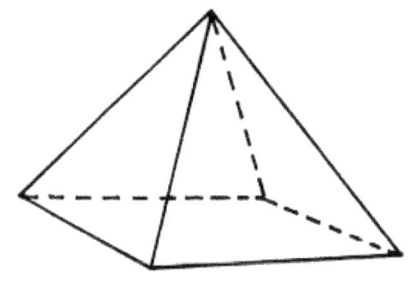

FIGURE 4: PYRAMID FOR THE FOUR BASIC ARCHETYPES

warrior is the *masochist,* so introverted as to be self-destructive while underhandedly abusive of others. We've all been cursed by *shadow* warrior energy but what about men and women dedicated to assertive expressions for the good of the whole; the gallant knightly expression of aggressive individuals driven by ambition but sensitive to justice, fair play, the rights of others and humanitarian causes, in other words to better the quality of life in our societies? Let's applaud true archetypal warrior energy of decisiveness and courage persevering against all enemies and loyal to a greater good beyond personal gain. Warrior is a vital part of our true expression!

The magician archetype in our make-up is wise to the point of being shrewd, able to step back in critical circumstances to access, magically, uncommon awareness with clever solutions to untenable situations – turning a sow's ear into a silk purse, as it were. The ultimate magician might be a revered sage or shaman. Of course without integrity this same uncanny ability can be used to manipulate people and situations in the self-serving ways of a *manipulator*, a shadow magician. A more underhanded and equally despicable magician in shadow is the *innocent one* who passively accesses wisdom to undermine others and their good intentions, taking personal advantage, deflating comrades if necessary and secretly lining his pockets and plans at others expense. When challenged he might say, "What did I do?" feigning innocence. Of course we're not just speaking of these archetypal forces in others. As our awareness grows of these forces at work in ourselv es we can choose to bring our magician qualities out of shadow so that they genuinely serve us and our fellows.

Our lover archetype is full of flair, color, artistry and romance. It brings "zing" into our lives. Lover is the underlying passion in us as we awaken to meet the challenges and delights awaiting us in a new day. Examples of lover energy in expression:

inner fullness – preparing and savoring a delicious meal after a stressful working day and fighting rush-hour traffic

a sense of peace – during our artistic endeavors with paints, flowers or hand-crafts while time seems to disappear

juicy delight – that candlelight dinner with someone we enjoy,

spiced with meaningful conversation and perhaps anticipation
of further closeness, etc., etc.

Make a list of *your* personal highlights relative to the artist and lover
within!

Lover archetypal energy is sensual and passionate, the libido
motivating force of the "four archetype" dynamic while the other three
in their calmness, strength and wisdom hold a poignant balance making
our life journey truly fulfilling and worthwhile. Without the constant
integrating "dance of the four quarters" (archetypes), key to a balanced
powerful expression, your lover energy will go into shadow as an
overwhelming force of addiction or gravitate toward impotence and
depression.

A negative shadow of any archetype will undermine clarity and
strength of the whole energetic foundation of our psyche. Can you see
results of these shadows taking form in our larger world – especially as
reported by media which tends to thrive on sensationalizing negativity,
human distortion, violence and destruction?

Health advocates encourage us to learn about our physical
anatomy and how it functions, inspiring personal hygiene, sensible
diet, exercise, etc. Such personal research increases our understanding,
influencing the choices we make in taking care of ourselves. A growing
awareness of the structure and function of our psyches will equip us
to make even better choices in our lives, not only crucial to physical
health but liberating our expression into the fullness of our potential.
I have begun to open the curtain on the mystery of the psyche in this
chapter. This understanding is not a head-trip but an opportunity to
access through feeling and observation those inherent qualities that will
bring our experience up to par with our highest vision. The psyche of

our Energy Field is vital, guiding us toward physical health and dynamic self-expression. The psyche's energetic and healing power can be uncovered by personal introspection, perhaps assisted by guidance from a counselor, psychologist, psychiatrist, spiritual mentor, knowing friend etc. Vibrational Healing releases restrictions in chakra flow for the body's healing which at the same time sets the mood for changes in our awareness and how we think. There are books and seminars combining new understanding with effective techniques. We learn by doing. What we discover with our minds is a starting point; what we know through feeling and doing makes the difference!

Leaders, Gurus, Religion

We began life on this planet as strangers in a strange land. For the first few days we were unable to focus our vision to see who or what was around us. It's hard for us to imagine now, let alone remember that experience. As well all sounds were strange; conscious thought and memory were apparently non-existent. As a newborn we perceived almost entirely through feeling. Apparently this feeling perception in a baby begins to develop early in the womb. In 1981 Dr. Thomas Verny published *The Secret Life Of The Unborn Child* which gave both mothers and fathers an unparalleled opportunity to connect with their unborn child. Even back then scientific studies could discern a responsive awareness in the child by the sixth month of pregnancy. Most of what is known with real authority – because it has been confirmed by physiological, neurological, biochemical, and psychological studies – is known about the child from the sixth month in utero (within the womb) onward. Apparently by that time we were a very sensitive human being. We could already remember, hear, even learn. It seems we were aware of repetitive rhythmic body sounds from our host, tones from her conversations, music that filtered through and other noises from the environment. All sound would be cushioned by the fluid medium surrounding us but no doubt we listened intently. We were a captive audience; what else was there to do? Initially we would have no reference point for whatever we heard or felt. It was a world known through some kind of pre-natal feeling perception. Research suggests that we were affected, comfortably or not, by what came through to us. Perhaps we were aware of things like this:

- how mother feels today – a pleasurable or uncomfortable current in her about the expanding fullness of my presence
- energy of delighted anticipation about my upcoming birth or fear, anger and resentment
- pleasing vibrations of her voice as she converses, especially during more intimate times with that "other one"
- her disturbed reactions from exposure to conflict, harshness and violence while watching TV or other occurrences in her/my environment.

And then the transition of birth, literally being pushed from our comfortable warm fluid nest through very confined spaces to eventually emerge into the non-fluid medium of cooler air, harsher sounds, touch from human hands, and hopefully comfort of breast, reassuring sounds and feelings of love at the end of the journey.

After birth infants hunger for love and enfoldment, a constant yearning as their bodies and minds are developing. They are keen to explore immediate sights, sounds and tactile perceptions of the world constantly coming more into view as their eyes are able to focus. In the early years almost everything is new and strange to emerging mental comprehension causing infants and children to look for touchstones, depending on adults to show the way to cope and understand. As a parent we may not realize how our every word, look, action and attitude is monitored closely by our children for the first years of their lives. That focus of attention on the parents likely wanes as the child grows, watching others, TV, etc., and before they reach their teens, involvement with peer groups will tend to have increasing impact on their behavior. Younger ones are mostly "feeling-sensitive", aware of our every whim and flush. They desperately look for leadership from our example and what we say to them in the thousand and one words of guidance and instruction. We are their first teachers, leaders, even gurus; their perception of our unspoken values and daily attitudes forms their way of life, their early religion.

It might seem we start our earth journey in a blank state knowing nothing. On the other hand we came with an inborn intelligence working through our personal Energy Field expanding and maintaining our trillions of cells working in harmony in thousands of physical chemical and mental processes. That same intelligence had drawn all our substance together sculpting our pre-birth form, seemingly for a purpose to be realized through our emerging unique expression over ensuing years. Perhaps within our innate intelligence is a depth of wisdom about who we are and what we came to bring, poised to unfold through our expression as our scope of awareness expands/evolves toward maturity. Comprehension of our inherent gifts and personal destiny emerge gradually, a process designed to continue revealing these secrets for the rest of our life, as long as we are open to them. Understanding can be stimulated by nature surrounding us, interactions with people and all challenges coming our way sometimes from every direction imaginable. Our genie of inherent wisdom uses all circumstances to increase our "world smarts" for survival and personal satisfaction. World smarts are a combination of becoming familiar with how the world around us works and an internal sensing of how to conduct ourselves most effectively; they could be called lessons in the art of living. Children often display wisdom beyond their years but so they don't have to reinvent the wheel every step of the way they look to others for clues in developing worldly skills as quickly as possible.

All keys from parents, siblings, relatives, elders, teachers and clergy don't have equal value. Some are helpful while others lead us down blind alleys and into difficulties but all can be learning experiences. Initially we may have trusted that all examples we saw and words of apparent wisdom were in our best interest but hopefully we learned to discern the wise from the foolish either through internal filtering or by surviving traumas from "the school of hard knocks". This self-discernment is crucial – the birth of honest skepticism penetrating the veil of innocent naivety. As we grew and learned we would feel a foundation of assurance and enthusiasm building, bringing a confidence to cope and flourish through life's diverse adventures. On the other hand harsh circumstances or personal abuse of one kind or another may have left us with a weak undergirding of fear and resentment as though walking on rough ground or on sinking sand – a sense of hopelessness about ever feeling that we would be of value. The other choice was to accept those jagged rocks of painful experience as prods to develop our backbone, stand our ground and find strength through adversity.

We are always looking for wise leadership to further our understanding of how things work in this world and to discover a moral base on which to build our values and our lives. This is not so with a sociopath who seems born convinced that the world is against him or her; nobody cares; it's a dog eat dog world. He's out to better himself by taking advantage of people and circumstances for his own ends regardless of who gets hurt in the process or what social rules are violated. He respects no social or spiritual authority other than his own – destructive skepticism. Such a person is not likely to be reading this book.

But while we are green (or open), we grow. Children have an insatiable hunger to discover meaning in mystery. They are fascinated with characters in children's books and mythical people in bible stories apparently finding enjoyment and moral direction from them – sometimes the more fantastic and surreal make deeper impressions on them like the Harry Potter series. We might wonder how they cope with violence and sadness mixed with humor and happy endings in stories, children's movies, TV cartoons and video games. They seem to take it all in stride, but do they? There are valid questions about deep emotional and cognitive complexity of a child's reactions to what they experience.

The greatest gift at any age is authentic leadership whether domestic, social, political, mentoring, social skills or inspiration from a spiritual leader, minister or guru. Authenticity implies a genuine expression of personal honesty and integrity, apparent in a person who shares freely what he thinks he knows while admitting he doesn't know it all. Someone's bold proclamation, "This is the absolute truth!" backed by some quoted myth or external authority causes me to shrink away from this shadow of ill-advised pronouncement. In order to learn anything new it is a natural first step to respect, trust and appreciate someone with expertise in a given field. However a human tendency is to put anyone on a pedestal who knows their subject well, especially someone who represents true understanding and reliability. It's not unusual for children or adults to idealize, project an aura of perfection, or even develop a crush on the one teaching them, be it parent, relative, teacher, sport coach or minister. Hopefully our view is conditioned over time realizing that he or she is not the perfect all knowing knight in shining armor or invincible wonder woman as they first appeared to us. This doesn't mean we lose respect for that person; just that it doesn't make sense to elevate anyone as an idol even if they are wise in a certain field. Realization should dawn that we are all flawed; none of us knows it all or lives a perfect life; we all need to continue learning, experiencing, growing in skill through a greater understanding of what life is all about. Often an adult with a need, perhaps in personal crisis, will idealize doctor, psychotherapist, minister/guru, boss or even a fresh unexplored specimen of the opposite sex. This inevitably leads to disillusion, hurt, a sense of loss, and may progress into bitterness and resentment, "Life is not fair!" On the other hand a responsible person in authority, or anyone receiving continuous adulation, needs to recognize this weakness in someone's response and be deliberate to refrain from projecting superiority. That will leave the onus for learning, healing and peace of mind upon the seeking one while using all available leadership skills and expertise to assist. One who is reveling in adulation received will become inflated with his own importance which in time will distort his perspective so that he teaches or leads unwisely. A wise mentor friend of mine says, "We're all hoboes on the same train", an expression referring to the dirty thirties of the depression when homeless men, princes and paupers alike, traveled together from place to place on trains in empty boxcars.

Questions about the ultimate mystery never seem to leave us: Who created the world? How? Where did I come from? Why am I here and where do I fit here on earth and in the larger scheme of things? What happens when I die? At any age we can choose to retain our youthful curiosity and inner vibrancy with an honest humility never losing the sense of awe in the larger mystery of which our personal mystery is part. How often it has been wisely said, "The more I know, the more I realize there is so much more that I don't know."

In primitive tribal groupings and more advanced early civilizations, individuals shared ideas about natural events like birth and death, day and night, the sun and moon, warmth and cold, storms, and other living things around them in attempts to put larger phenomena into personal perspective. A religion of sorts would form and pass down by word of mouth over generations. The nature of the lore developed would provide a sense of confidence about matters seemingly understandable and respect about others too large to comprehend. Religion today is defined: *a set of beliefs concerning the cause, nature, and purpose of the universe, especially when considered as the creation of a superhuman agency or agencies usually involving devotional and ritual observances, and often containing a moral code for the conduct of human affairs*. These sets of beliefs serve to guide a child or a seeking person of any age into some understanding of how things work and what's expected of them – a sense of morals and a code of conduct. This is not only useful for an individual's sense of confidence but serves to maintain a reasonable control and coordination within a group of people, what could be called a "civil"ization. However a combination of power hunger on the part of a few and the tendency to follow blindly in many tends to set patterns of behavior not always conducive to true self-realization of the individual. For example, we may be taught to follow a certain code of conduct in accordance with religious doctrine in order to insure our future after death. We may be called upon to worship certain prophets or saviors in order to be a good person and receive their spiritual support in our endeavors. We may develop a false sense of humility as being less than those who lead us or even feeling gross inferiority as miserable sinners having to grovel for some sense of worthiness. A religious leader by any name may be deemed infallible, not to be questioned at the risk of finding one self marginalized, excommunicated or in some cases killed. While all this may be vital in developing a strong church, synagogue or mosque, locally or worldwide, what does it do to an individual's sense of self and personal value as a human being, born unique with special gifts to offer into the whole fabric of humanity and larger world? I am reminded of words of C.G. Jung: *His Myth In Our Time*, by M.L. Franz:

> *Even a small group is ruled by a suggestive group-spirit which,*
> *if it is good, can have very favorable social effects, although*
> *at the cost of the spiritual and moral independence of the*
> *individual. The group enhances the ego, which is to say that*
> *one becomes bolder, more adapted, more secure, more*
> *impudent and less prudent while the self is diminished and*
> *shoved into the background in favor of the average.*

Religions need not be exclusively spiritual. Today's religions of academia and science wield considerable power over people. It has been said that all wars are religious wars with one faction pitted against the other to the glory of their particular "god" but actually for the benefit of those who hold the power on the winning side. A projected mythical image, savior, or knight in shining armor may be of value as an example setting a standard of conduct but it is not your reality. Your personal reality already exists and as you begin to hear the beat of that drummer, tread your adventurous path in trust, you will access inner tonal guidance individual to you. A mentor, idol or celebrity may bring the gift of inspiration but no one is qualified to tell you what to do, where to go or how to do it – just you!

New Levels of Perception

The understanding of extra-sensory perception has changed considerably over the years. On the one hand people are fascinated with unusual sensitivity and practices spanning from the paranormal to the occult. We pay performers to dazzle us with supernatural abilities; we read science-fiction, watch movies and TV shows in that genre. At the same time we judge as strange anyone or any group of people whose beliefs and lifestyles are different from our own. When people we know demonstrate visions and practices that vary from what we consider acceptable, not validated by methods of science or general acceptance of the time, they are ridiculed, marginalized and persecuted. If someone claims some outlandish sensitivity or skill I'm liable to criticize and resent them. If what they do violates a social or religious taboo of mine I might say they're insane or evil. These attitudes are directed toward fortunetellers, soothsayers, prophets, healers, spoon-benders, levitators, those who speak with the deceased or can see ghosts – and the list goes on. Women with paranormal powers, whether thought to be for good or evil, were called witches and burned at the stake just a couple of centuries ago. Warlocks, their male counterparts were also feared and dealt with inhumanely. Today we might be more informed and slightly more tolerant.

As examples:

- Someone looks at a pregnant woman or uses a pendulum to tell what sex the child will be.

- Indigenous people of a region predict how severe or mild next winter will be.

- Sailors still forecast weather by colors in the sky, evening and morning, but a few centuries back they would of necessity navigate their ships by the stars, a feat beyond most of us landlubbers today.

If someone's unusual perceptions are accurate enough that they can't be repudiated we call them extra-sensory. Are they really "extra" or evidence of sensitivity available to many of us that we've never accessed? Are our inabilities genetic, a trick of fate or the result of de-sensitizing through our passion to be normal and socially acceptable? Most of us were driven from an early age, subconsciously or by observation to be "normal", to conform to family protocol and blend with our social flock, grasping at personal meaning through a sense of belonging. As children we learned, sometimes the hard way, not to rock the boat – to keep under wraps questionable perceptions and experiences that "never should be mentioned". Hasn't this pressure to stay within an acceptable scope of awareness stunted our willingness to perceive things beyond what we thought possible? Could we not open ourselves to untapped abilities rather than holding to limited views and values deemed normal to our fellows? Perhaps we can grow to understand more about the nature of our mind's invisible connections within our own Energy Field, linking us to each other and to the world around us – to have a keener awareness of the vastness and power of nature – to go where few have gone before. Let's expand our horizons inspired by those who are already breaking through barriers in ventures we feel attracted to.

Mind covers a whole range of mental and emotional perception with varying depths of feeling from hunches to spiritual sensitivity. In the broadest sense of mind/ awareness we receive information, sense possibilities, envision, dream or daydream and form thoughts to ponder or live by. All of this comes by means of the medium of our Energy Field through our heart and mind just as all our internal physical functions are supported and coordinated through the same medium, as if by magic. (See chapter *The 24/7 Genie – always on the job*) According to older Newtonian scientific thinking we assume our minds are confined to our brains. Our brains are essential to conscious awareness of course, just as cell phones, television sets, radios and computers convert invisible waves and frequencies into words, sounds and pictures. The brain is a biological instrument, we might say the ultimate multi-dimensional computer, playing a part in the larger awareness of what we call mind. This field of awareness is as evident all through the body as it is in the head. When you stub your big toe, the perception of pain registers neurologically in this organ in your head, yet you know exactly where your injury has taken place – "my toe hurts." You see something ugly and disgusting with your eyes and immediately your whole sensory system reacts and you feel effects perhaps in your stomach area. Your mental/ awareness channel, the mind, can connect your thoughts to Fields in which other minds exist. Connections transmitted and received through the invisible medium of human Energy Fields make telepathy and many other phenomena possible, whether they seem strange or common place. We've been brainwashed that each of us is a separate individual. Yet it is often proclaimed, "We are all one; we are interconnected with our fellow humans and ultimately with all of creation." This lofty viewpoint, religious or philosophical, is now being validated by leading-edge scientists engaged in quantum physics research.

A substantial report on the latest hard evidence from these pioneering scientists is compiled by Lynne McTaggart in her book, *The Field, The Quest for the Secret Force of the Universe*:

> *For a number of decades respected scientists in a variety of disciplines all over the world have been carrying out well-designed experiments whose results fly in the face of current biology and physics...*
>
> *What they have discovered is nothing less than astonishing. At our most elemental, we are not a chemical reaction, but an energetic charge. Human beings and all living things are a coalescence of energy in a field of energy connected to every other thing in the world. This pulsating energy field is the central engine of our being and our consciousness, the alpha and the omega of our existence. There is no "me" and "not me" duality to our bodies in relation to the universe, but one underlying energy field...*
>
> *The field, as Einstein once succinctly put it, is the only reality.*

It might be shocking to consider your personal Bio-Field in constant contact with the fields of others as well as animals and vegetation in the larger Field we call nature, the whole energetic mesh. Our inability to perceive and acknowledge impressions received from beyond ourselves may be due to biases from our background but a willingness to face our inner restrictions can free us to reach "out of the box" beyond common awareness to expand our sensitivity. These inter-field connections are active anyway affecting us in various ways we're not aware of. Can we become conscious of them? As we become more aware, what seemed to be extra-sensory becomes normal to us. There are many examples we take for granted illustrating energetic charges moving between resonant fields, i.e. fields that vibrate on the same frequency or even overlap.

Here are a few:

- Have you noticed that you can't stare at a person without that person eventually feeling your energetic intrusion and looking directly back at you with a questioning look even if you were staring at the back of their head in a crowd or they were some distance away from you?

- While walking down the street feeling up-beat you happen to meet an acquaintance, share a few surface pleasantries and then wonder moments after you leave them why you've suddenly picked up uncomfortable feelings that stay with you and may even disturb you the rest of your day.

- The phone rings and you know who it is before you answer, or while you're thinking about someone they phone you.

- You feel foreboding about a close friend or relative only to find out later that they were involved in an accident or died at that time.

- If you have a pet dog or cat, how do they sense you're about to arrive home, waiting in the place they always do even when it's not your regular time to return or you've been away for an extended time?

Biologist Dr. Rupert Sheldrake in *The Sense Of Being Stared At* and *Dogs That Know When Their Owners Are Coming Home* writes about many of these common but unnoticed events and reports from his research of *social fields*. Social fields can sometimes be called morphogenetic fields, resonant patterns that link animals, insects and birds together – each within their own species. These fields activate and coordinate their activities without need for outer communication between individuals of one species. There is mounting evidence with humans that as more and more people learn about or master a new activity it becomes easier for others to do it, almost without thinking. Many of us over 60 are astounded to see young children move into cell phone use and computer skills without a second thought, free of difficult learning curves we suffer approaching similar technology. Here are some examples beyond the human experience:

- All bees in a hive, not just the queen bee, know immediately when it's time to swarm and seek out a new home. Ants or termites in their respective colonies work together like clockwork to build and maintain their nests.

- Wolves of a pack may have miles between them at times but are always aware of each others presence and position.

- It's astounding to watch hundreds of sandpipers in a flock feeding in the sand at the seashore suddenly all take flight as one unit, sometimes making turns of 90 to 180 degrees, ascending and descending together at great speed only to land in silence together in a new foraging location without ever colliding or touching each other. Notice this is all accomplished without guidance from air traffic controllers who coordinate aircraft flights with sophisticated electronic equipment on the ground and in the planes, as is necessary in the human world.

- When one group of animals or birds discovers a new skill,

its practice appears simultaneously throughout that same grouping all over the world. People refer to The Hundredth Monkey Syndrome: a herd of macaques on an island in the Pacific discovered when their sweet potatoes fell into water by accident, they tasted better; other macaques on islands separated by ocean all began to wash their sweet potatoes before eating. There was a phenomenon in Britain in the 1960s of Blue Tits, local garden birds, who seemed to learn instantaneously as a wide-spread group how to penetrate the foil caps protecting British milk bottles on window sills to get at the cream underneath.

When radio was invented, Marconi, Tesla, Armstrong and De Forest were all on the same edge of discovery and the man who got the patent first got the credit – and subsequently became rich. This was also true of Alexander Graham Bell, Meucci and Gray, opening up communication by telephone at the same time. Chiropractic through Daniel Palmer and Osteopathy through Andrew Still brought out similar manipulation techniques of human spinal columns circa 1895. Each man had a different theory of how their techniques produced beneficial results for their patients. Rather than it being the inventor thinking up ideas in his brain, consider it as a charged impulse moving through his social field penetrating his personal Energy Field and the Fields of others similarly attuned. Conscious recognition comes to the mind and then comes research and development to transform inspiration into a useful or saleable product. Discoveries often appear by accident while in pursuit of something else. Financial backing and legal expertise are vital for the inspired object to become a successful product. The question is: where did the initial impulse come from and how did it penetrate conscious awareness?

Considering human social fields there is no better (or worse) example than destructiveness erupting among spectators at a sporting event or a social protest when many caught in the wave of the moment act insanely, beyond their personal character and integrity. A mob probably set off by one or two people becomes an instantaneous violent social field. Conversely the majority of people in society follow unwritten standards of conduct without being conscious of who set the pattern, if indeed anyone did. It seems there is a reasonable way to behave in situations and most of us "sense" what that is. Rupert Sheldrake at the IONS conference in 2007 said,

> *"[T]here's a kind of intention, a kind of goal-directedness inherent in the very nature of life in the most fundamental processes that enable embryos to grow and even protein molecules to form. And I think that the kind of conscious intention we experience as part of our mental life has its background in this goal-directedness which is inherent in all living creatures, and is an essential part of the nature of life and an essential part of the nature of the organizing fields that organize living organisms".*

The news media of course constantly highlight and sensationalize exceptions, to the point where we might think chaos and disaster is the normal state of affairs for the majority of people most of the time. Within the social field of driving a car for example, I'm amazed at how few accidents there are considering the number of drivers on the road, speed of travel, diversity of skill and varied conditions of cars. Even more in question are the mental/ emotional states of some drivers because of non-related problems and stresses that can't help but impinge on their ability to operate a vehicle safely. Generally there is a flow to traffic far beyond our conscious ability to make it happen – you might call it a social field positively influencing most people involved. Yes there are accidents, unlike sandpipers in flight, but they are exceptions rather than the rule. Otherwise insurance rates would be so high as to be prohibitive. Take a personal poll: for the number of auto trips you take, city and highway, how often do you have a motor vehicle accident? What percentage would that be – and is that because you are a perfect driver? If you think you are, take another driving test and see how you score.

My own discovery of non-touch healing required setting aside my chiropractic protocol when I discovered a new sensitivity – my initial awareness of people's energy fields. In practice my partner and I had used analytical instruments to locate persistent pressure on nerves in and around the spinal cord. We would consult over these readings often requiring 2 or 3 visits of a patient to reach a conclusion. Then we'd x-ray the offending area of the spine to discover the vertebral distortion causing the pressure. Only then would we administer one or more vertebral adjustments to relieve nerve interference, in the person's best interest. What surprised us on occasion was a remarkable release of a patient's symptoms before we had given the first corrective adjustment. For example, a man in his 60s came to see us in great distress reporting persistent pain in his abdomen for 10 years. On his second visit he said to me, "Doctor, I don't know what you've done but since my first visit a few hours ago I've had an amazing release of the pain. Thank you!" What a shock! To our awareness at that time we hadn't done anything but run tests. Examples like this awakened us to other levels of interchange affecting our patients besides our chiropractic treatment. Also we became aware of energy currents in our hands and sensed distinct vibratory exchanges between doctor and patient that assisted the release of an internal power of correction and healing in their bodies. Over time our sensitivity increased making us aware of the most effective areas in their energetic fields where we could apply our vibratory currents to good advantage. I became aware of distinct layers of energy around each person as well as specific power points around their endocrine/hormonal centers which eventually led me to recognize primary power centers in a body's field. These centers had been named "chakras" in eastern philosophies and healing. I had opportunity as well to learn from people who had experience with these things and there were helpful books to read. As my understanding and my practice continued to evolve I coined the term Vibrational Healing: the interchange of vibratory frequencies to balance and clarify another individual's Energy Field releasing natural healing power within them.

Once the door to increasing sensitivity is ajar, it keeps opening further and "extra" sensitivity enhances perception. Sometimes it's called expanding our 6th sense; people becoming more intuitive, empathic or even spiritual, realizing at a deeper level how much more we have to offer into our living expression. But wherever we are in our expanding awareness, there is always so much more to learn and experience. To paraphrase an old biblical saying, "Eye has not seen, nor ear heard, nor sensitivity opened, neither has it entered into the awareness of men and women, things life's magic has yet in mind for those willing to transcend their limiting beliefs for personal good and to benefit others." Extra-sensory discoveries coming out of our personal Biofield are an adventure in expanded living and increased understanding, well worth the effort.

Instinct-Intuition-Insight

We usually relate instinct to animals, who carry a built-in wisdom that people don't possess. It's a broad-spectrum know-how covering predictable needs and functions as well as challenges that can appear in the moment. A new mother of any species inherently knows what to do as birth drama unfolds. Where should she nest, how to relax into muscular contractions that are bringing offspring out of her body, how and when to sever umbilical cords, clean up her pups/kittens, encourage them to nurse her milk and how to protect them? If she births by eggs, she also has to be willing to be fertilized by the male at just the right time, build a nest hopefully with her partner's help, settle long enough to lay the eggs, keep them at the right temperature and turn them periodically in the nest until the newborns emerge. What courses do these so called dumb creatures study to learn about their specific routine of procreation and how to cooperate with each phase without anyone to teach or guide them? Isn't it amazing? That's just a small part of their whole field of instinctual knowing and inner guidance. How does an animal know what to eat, what's good food and what's poison? Where is the best water source? When and where to hunt for food? Whether to climb trees or dig a burrow? Threatened by a predator, how do they know whether to fight or flee, and did they develop this wisdom with parents, playing with siblings, the school of hard knocks, or is some of it just there instinctively? We do the magic of life-in-action a disservice when we say, "Oh well, it's just instinct!"

Sir Laurens van der Post, in the 1980s, wrote about his successful face-to-face interaction with a rhinoceros in South Africa, where he could have been killed. He explained why that animal had become such an important symbol to him. He also mentioned his appreciation for the keener sense of smell all animals have than we do. From his *A Walk With A White Bushman*:

So the sense of smell in animals is what intuition is to the human spirit. It tells you of the invisible, of what cannot be detected by other means. It tells you things that are not there, yet are coming. You see into the blind opaque past and round the corner of time. It is the smell of things to come, of intuition, on which man's capacity for creation depends. And I think myself, you see, the act of creation is very sudden – it may be building up there in the dark. But when it happens, it happens like a flash of lightning. Life has taken a leap forward. But intuition is the vision in creation and the human spirit that leaps into the dark and, through the dark, into unknown areas of itself and life. There is an old saying, look before you leap. Wait until you can see, and then leap. But then perhaps you never leap at all. Intuition is the leap forward to creation when all other senses fail and would arrest it. So that intuition is the most vital element, I think, of all the instincts we have inherited. This impels man to leap into the unknown, into new areas of awareness that he has not discovered before.

I do not know what it is, but I do know that, without looking for it, one is aware of something more...a feeling of something

*being prepared in the future when there is nothing around
to explain that anything of the kind is happening. In fact, the
whole of one's development at a given moment may point in
the opposite direction, and yet one is aware that his direction
is false, and that way over the horizon something is preparing
an introduction into one's life, a pattern of planning beyond the
law of cause and effect. I think my whole life demonstrates it:
my life has not been planned, I have always taken what was on
my doorstep… and yet looking back on it, more and more it
has a definite shape, a pattern as if planned in advance.*

Considering the way we generally live, where intuition and extra-sensory perception are rarely acknowledged, we might see that it's not enough to live up to the expectations of society, gleaned from our education, indoctrination and experience. Through a large part of our years of training and formal education toward adulthood from kindergarten and before, we sense, "This is what is expected of you – how to be a responsible person – acceptable by the larger "us" or even by a greater deity!" We may feel a specific obligation from a parent, a partner, a lover, colleagues or close friends. But a life so lived following the party line, the status quo – so called accepted values – often leads us to personal dissatisfaction, frustration, even depression – and the challenging question, "Is this all there is to my life?" To compensate for feeling poorly about ourselves we are susceptible to a wide spectrum of addictions: physical, chemical and psychological. A popular addictive practice is idealizing celebrities: actors, athletes, musicians, authors, political and religious leaders, becoming dependent on drawing meaning by basking in someone else's glory. What about our own sense of meaning? "Where is my life going and does it really count

in the larger picture?" We can look around at examples of people
who have broken out of the box of current knowledge and social
expectations to bring forth something new into all our lives. Through a
fineness of intuition sometimes called spiritual insight, a new invention,
a useful product, a new idea of a more successful way to personal
fulfillment or just a simple novel way to change our lives, is brought into
form to the betterment of ourselves and the larger community we live
in.

It's intriguing that when a new invention does break through in
consciousness it often emerges through more than one person at the
same time. An individual will be engaged in research propelled by a
sensing, an intuition, unaware that someone in the next county or half
way around the world is following the same hunch.

We all hear many internal voices: of personal inadequacy –
expectations from others – recurring feelings from past experiences
– uncertainty about the future, etc. Our intuitive or soul voice is
a different frequency and has a unique tone often drowned out
by incessant information chatter bombarding us. During a healing
experience, meditation, dreaming or even daydreaming, a person may
touch into this higher frequency. We can sharpen our fine tuning in
this regard by exercising our ability to listen in normal circumstances.
In conversation for example, do you concentrate on what a person is
saying, words and feelings, or are you preoccupied with your opinions
and what you'll say back to them? Or, "I don't have time – he or she is
not important – it's going to rain – that's a nice car or attractive person
who just went by." Listening is an art to be developed through exercise
opening the way for a keener ear to one's own voice of intuition. That
takes silence, a state that many of us find uncomfortable. Take this

opportunity to listen to your body and the inner space behind – above – between all our cells, organs and systems. This powerful matrix of invisible bio-energy contains the magic of our existence and may be perceived as a powerful tone of clear vibration.

It is much simpler for an animal to be on his special wavelength and to stay there, guided by inner wisdom we call instinct; there aren't so many of the distractions that we are subject to. In order to tune into our inherent dynamic wavelength we call intuition or insight we must master more evolved complex mental, emotional and spiritual capabilities of the human psyche. We talk about the wonder of multi-tasking mentally and physically; women are often touted as being more adept at this than men. Project that into the task of processing the unbelievable amount of visual, audible and invisible stimuli coming at us constantly and expanding exponentially with today's technology. Can we do this without losing our primary connection with the constant source of personal guidance and sense of inner confidence available through intuition? Can we put into perspective all that comes to us and sense the way to unique and fertile thoughts and actions? Not just for our own enhancement and understanding but to the benefit of this wonderful earthly and cosmic ecosystem where we have the privilege of living?

Instinct is the natural guidance for animals, producing so many wonders in Nature. We can choose to open ourselves intuitively, through heart and mind, to achieve marvels in what we do. There is a pressing need for this growth toward our greater understanding to encompass the explosion of technology and information in our world; even now it is more than our minds can grasp and assimilate. A constant flow of inspiration in enough people may induce common sense, clarity and a true spiritual/moral viewpoint to pervade and coordinate human activity. Knowledge and technological ability do not equal wisdom in action. Where there is no vision, the people perish! There is no magic potion or cosmic switch to instantly propel all humankind to its optimum awareness. It will happen by choice, one person at a time who is sensitive and open to the amazing sanity and wisdom inherent in the Field. You and I are the only ones to consider at the moment and only "I" can take the steps to greater insight.

Individuation and the Soul's Code

A friend sent me an e-mail of Planet Earth: colored satellite photos scanning our earth, a globe in space, views of continents and oceans as the sun moves across leaving night behind while its line of light magically moves from east to west. The night time illuminations of large populated areas are visible in their various locations. It's awesome and breathtaking! This beautiful moving sphere is where we live at present. How did we get here and why? What does it all mean? How easy it is with our every day distractions to forget this breathtaking cosmic landscape of which we're a part and let details of our busyness overshadow our potential meaning in the larger picture – a mystery you have likely questioned as I have. I wonder if our journey on this magnificent planet, as limited as it is in time, suggests we've come here from another dimension of creative interplay – a place we might return when our time here is up?

Do you ever question?

- Why am I here?
- Why did I incarnate and birth into this particular race, that specific family, in this part of the world? Was that part of my earth commission giving me just the obstacles, challenges, and support needed to draw out who I am and further my ongoing growth?
- Were these decisions made at another level and was I directly involved?
- Is timing of my presence here of particular significance in the

larger world picture – or happenstance?

As infant or young child it's likely we did not remember the above questions or have concern about answers. We start with a relatively blank slate of awareness and look to our parents or primary caregivers for a sense of belonging and meaning. We carry similar hereditary factors as our parents making it easy to resonate with them, albeit unconsciously. Depending on their ease and love, we felt secure and at home. If primary caregivers were outside family you probably didn't identify as easily with them but you were looking for it anyway; love and acceptance is a welcome gift from anyone. As we moved toward our teens a more definite longing for identity emerged and we hungered to feel more like a person in our own right. We wanted to be seen as a unique individual, distinctly ourselves at a time when peer acceptance tended to replace earlier needs for approval we sought from our parents. Pursuit of individuality can be a driving force through adolescence constantly testing authority and status quo, in our minds if not through our overt expression. Individualism asserted its pressure in different ways as we moved toward adulthood amidst constant inner questioning or demands from others about what we are going to do with our lives – training, education and career are great concerns. This push to be our self continued to haunt us complicated by dynamic of relationships, possibly marriage and children and the urge to achieve a semblance of success and financial stability among our siblings and peers. It's not unusual to be consumed our whole lives for a place in the social scene as a distinct and worthwhile individual. Eventually we reach whatever status we have in our own eyes and among our fellows. Then mid-life crisis comes along. What have I done? Is it satisfying? Is this all life is about? Where do I go from here?

Reaching our sixties with children grown and on their own, my wife and I saw our combined careers in one service-oriented organization dissolve, no longer carrying our vision or passion. Starting out to recreate ourselves, careers and all, we felt compelled to trade our comfortable family sedan for a convertible sports car – to appease our anxiety by being "out to play" in a way we would never have considered before in our responsible positions. As well as easing feelings of frustration and despair it was great fun and we drove a convertible for 15 years. Mid-life crises are not always so simple and tidy and they occur anywhere between 35 and whatever age. They are a dramatic response to inner questioning and dissatisfaction with whatever heights we have or have not achieved. It seems individualistic strivings, accomplishments or the lack thereof, leave us hungering for something more. A passion for "more" at this vulnerable period may drive a person into compulsive, illogical, self-destructive actions, often involving dramatic shifts in attitude and action toward sex or money, leaving friends, associates, spouse and family aghast, wondering whatever possessed this reasonable person to go off the rails and do such inane things. Mid-life antics can destroy a reputation, end a job or prestigious position, destroy a marriage and leave a family in ruin. It seems this powerful compulsion is no respecter of person, sex or age. What a mid-life crisis marks is a new challenge to search for deeper meaning. If we succumb to these urges without discovering what's behind them we may end up down the road angry, frustrated or even bitter, without really knowing why. What's seeking to come out like a second birth is a new sense of meaning and purpose – called *individuation*, a longing for a Self greater than the self-identity we have known.

James Hollis, a psychologist, describes this process in his book, *Finding Meaning in the Second Half of Life – How to Finally Really Grow Up*:

> *Just what are those imperatives that rise to support us*
> *and challenge us in the journey of the second half of life?*
> *Perhaps Jung's most compelling contribution is the idea of*
> ***individuation****, that is the lifelong project of becoming more*
> *nearly the whole person we were meant to be – what the*
> *gods intended, not the parents, or the tribe, or, especially, the*
> *easily intimidated or inflated ego. While revering the mystery*
> *of others, our individuation summons each of us to stand in*
> *the presence of our own mystery, and become more fully*
> *responsible for who we are in this journey we call our life. So*
> *often the idea of individuation has been confused with self-*
> *indulgence or mere individualism, but what individuation more*
> *often asks of us is the surrender of the ego's agenda of security*
> *and emotional reinforcement in favor of humbling service to*
> *the soul's intent. This is quite the opposite of self-indulgence;*
> *it is the service of the ego to the higher order manifested to us*
> *through the Self.*

We think we know ourselves but that self may be more a product from early indoctrination than the genuine entity inherent at our birth. We believe we are a certain type of person, with set morals and values and definite qualities of character. On closer examination we may find these attributes have been determined by our social field, by our parents whether we wanted to emulate them or not, by unwritten codes and ways of thinking of our friends, by values our education and vocation demand in order to be a success. Whether company president, doctor, minister, clerk, salesperson, craft-person, homemaker, etc., the setting we were raised in and now live, including our vocation(s), exert pressure upon our individual field of behavior and over time molds our character so successfully we become convinced that's the way we are. "I've always been this way!" "That's the way I think!" "My feelings are always aroused this way when that person or situation presents itself – that's the way I am and nothing can change that." "I am definitely this type of person and don't try to tell me differently!" In short we are so blinded by defensiveness relative to how we think we are and what other people might think about us. Thus, we fail to see the opportunity for further growth, denying ourselves a new adventure to discover more of our real Self. But this venture will require deeper honesty in your own thinking through quiet meditation, journaling, dream analysis, vibrational healing perhaps assisted by wise counsel, taking the opportunity to look at your self in a new way as if you're watching a movie of someone else's life.

As you uncover your past in an objective way you may be surprised at many influences that have directed your actions and development: early family experiences, teachers, accidents, illnesses, close friends, crushes, romances, successes, failures, disappointments, deaths, etc. In retrospect these influences may seem positive or negative. Old feelings of anger, sadness, resentment or deep pleasure and joyfulness may be revived. In fact you may see all events of your life connected by a litany of feelings, like glue holding the fabric of your experience in one continuous garment – your coat of many colors. It takes a good measure of reflective honesty, what is often called "personal work", to do this but how freeing it is to face these things straight-on without continuing to hold blame against anyone. Here's the opportunity to view events of your past and see everyone involved, including you, was doing the best they knew how according to their personal viewpoints at that time and in those specific circumstances.

Emerging through the mists of your memories and feelings can be a realization of a daimon present in you who, beyond genetics and circumstances or even your conscious intention, has been pushing to show itself and direct your path. James Hillman writes about this daimon in *The Soul's Code – In Search of Character and Calling*:

There is more in a human life than our theories of it allow. Sooner or later something seems to call us onto a particular path. You may remember this "something" as a signal moment in childhood when an urge out of nowhere, a fascination, a peculiar turn of events struck like an annunciation: This is what I must do, this is what I've got to have. This is who I am.

If not this vivid or sure, the call may have been more like gentle pushings in the stream in which you drifted unknowingly to a particular spot on the bank. Looking back, you sense that fate had a hand in it.

The soul of each of us is given a unique daimon before we are born, and it has selected an image or pattern that we live on earth. This soul-companion, the daimon, guides us here; in the process of arrival, however, we forget all that took place and believe we come empty into this world. The daimon remembers what is in your image and belongs to your pattern, and therefore your daimon is the carrier of your destiny.

In Hillman's book he uses many examples of prominent people we may have heard about. For instance young Ella Fitzgerald at 16 enters Amateur Night at the Harlem Opera House. She is announced as she had chosen – to dance. However she changes her mind at the last moment and informs the master of ceremonies that she is going to sing. Ella goes on to become a famous jazz singer. Yehudi Menuhin the world-renowned violinist wanted a violin for his fourth birthday but was very upset when his parents bought him a toy violin; he would have nothing to do with it. Franklin Roosevelt, President of the U.S. in the 1930s to the early 40s, sensed something special about 28 year old Lyndon Johnson from Texas and said to a colleague, "In the next couple of generations the balance of power in this country is going to shift to the South and the West. And that kid Lyndon Johnson could well be the first Southern President." Johnson was inaugurated after the assassination of President John Kennedy in 1963 and was subsequently re-elected for a second term.

C.G. Jung a pioneering psychiatrist born in the 19th century, whose major contributions are associated with the 20th century, died in 1961. He devoted his life developing what has become one of the foundation stones of modern psychology. In his book *Memory, Dreams, Reflection*, from his later years:

> *I have had much trouble getting along with my ideas. There was a daimon in me, and in the end its presence proved decisive. It overpowered me, and if I was at times ruthless it was because I was in the grip of the daimon. I could never stop at anything once attained. I had to hasten on, to catch up with my vision. Since my contemporaries, understandably, could not perceive my vision, they saw only a fool rushing ahead.*
> *A creative person has little power over his own life. He is not free. He is captive and driven by his daimon.*

Of course this mission of the soul is present in all of us and perhaps you can see its blueprint pushing through as you look back and separate your genetic and developed characteristics – who you think you are – from a distinct quality and sense of destiny that is as singular to you as your voice and fingerprint. How hidden or available this character will be depends on internal listening and the choices we make. Personally my outer human character would rather have conformed to experience success within the status quo. However I could not but follow the dictates coming through my heart, from I knew not where. My planned direction toward a medical career changed 90 degrees when I entered chiropractic with great enthusiasm; then later in practice I awoke with a passion for healing through energy and vibration. It hasn't always been easy to walk my path but it is mine and I'm happy in it. I had never considered writing a book but I can feel my daimon pushing line by line, giving me a sense of inner satisfaction. Each of us has a constant challenge, an ultimate opportunity, to individuate – to be our Self rather than follow the status quo, or herd mentality.

With you is a *daimon*, a special talent – a gift to be expressed. When you are dedicated to clarify existing limitations within your personal Energy Field and disregard other people's expectations, as well as your own, you are free to explore your unique birthright.

Soft Listening and the Silent Mind

To achieve soft listening and the silent mind may sound esoteric, indeed wishful thinking, in the pace and complexity of today's world. It may seem as though such an accomplished level of sensitive awareness is reserved for spiritually endowed folks in protected settings perhaps having benefited from special training. Yes, it is a matter of attaining a sufficient skill level seemingly out of reach for most of us if our vision is limited to coping with challenges of survival living. But there are many stages to developing a skill whether artistic, athletic, academic or social. A professional athlete doesn't start at the top but undergoes intensive training, study and hard work to develop and refine abilities he or she may have been born with – it is similar with mastering any skill. Coping is one of the first steps; mastery is further down the line of persistent application and growth. In this chapter I address a number of challenges and methods involved in increasing the skill level of the mind and heart toward a foundation of heightened awareness. I begin with the assumption of the inherent potential in each of us. Just as good physical health is possible by accessing the frequencies of our Bio-Energy Field, mental and emotional health hinges on learning to attune more precisely to our larger presence existing through that same Field.

If you are asked, "What do you really want?" or "What moves you most deeply?" – you might easily name happiness, relationship, health, wealth, success, etc. Perhaps these are on the surface of a mountain of less visible relatively unconscious wants, desires or fantasies driving you day and night, either to realize those hidden desires or to cause internal discomfort from frustration of dreams unrealized. Below the surface, your deeper "wants" are not impossible to bring to conscious light with a little prodding in conversation or honest personal journaling. It is important to acknowledge hidden desires for pleasures and satisfactions held in so long they seem forgotten but still exist somewhere in the depth of your psyche. Keeping these dreams hidden sets them up as goals we are not able to achieve; such closeted beliefs not being recognized have considerable influence on how we think and act today and what we achieve or not. In addition to these internal disturbances, influences also exist from the pack we run with in our personal world – competitions and judgments with family, job, and social connections.

Characteristic of the 21st century we are beset by increasing noise: music, conversations, sirens, news broadcasts, crowds, traffic, etc. Sounds of nature are still around us even in the middle of a city and can be very nourishing if we take time to hear them. In order to maintain our sanity to do what's in front of us we tune out many sounds but all are received in our Bio-Energy Field and affect our heads, our hearts and our physical well-being. We can be so accustomed to the cacophony that we dread silence, needing radio or TV playing when we're alone just for company. Inaudible pressures surround us too: unspoken thoughts from others or our own busy minds: "Why are they looking at me that way? How do they feel about me? Why am I always so tired? Will I ever be able to pay the bills? Is this all there is to my life?" And there's constantly increasing silent high frequency "noise" floating around us, more than we imagine: vibrations from cell phone transmission, TV and radio signals, computers and other electronic devices.

The total field of awareness we call mental is a busy complex space with constant input adding to our reservoir of alive or buried feelings, memories from the past, ambitions fulfilled or shattered, pain and heartache. It's all we can do at times to cope with escalating busyness, from within or from without, let alone begin to make sense of it all. What doesn't happen in our waking moments comes up in our dreams. Interesting perspectives on this constant inner chatter are reported by those who have experienced time in a sensory deprivation tank. Harry Palmer in *Living Deliberately* writes about his experience in such a tank for the purpose of discovering how the mind works:

The tank was a hardened polystyrene foam chamber about eight feet long and four feet square. It contained a solution of water with 800 pounds of Epsom salts dissolved in it. The water is so saturated with salt that your body floats effortlessly. You lose any sense of gravity. The temperature is brought up to the same temperature as your skin, around 94 degrees, so there is no sense of hot or cold. It is neutral. The tank is so dark that you can't tell if your eyes are open or closed. The tank is also soundproof.

When you are in the tank, you float weightlessly; there is no sense of feel, no sense of sound, no perception. You are just there, in consciousness, deprived of external sensation and present time experience.

For the next eight weeks, I spent most of my time in the tank. The only evidence of my existence was the dried Epsom salt trails leading to the refrigerator and the bathroom. "Happy trails".

One of the first things that becomes evident during sensory deprivation is that the mind is more than willing to compensate for any lack of sensory input. Sensory input actually keeps the mind somewhat in focus and under control, like wet-sheet wrapping someone who is severely disturbed.

When the body's sensory input is deprived, the mind compensates and becomes a three-ring circus with steam calliopes, high school marching bands and auctioning contests. It is a chaotic experience that somehow you must rise through to reach the stillness beyond mind.

What of the question of "stillness beyond mind", the purpose of the float tank for many who use it? Your Bio-Energy Field is a large sphere of multi-frequency vibrations. These vibrations translate themselves into thought and action through a physical organ called the brain – the fountainhead of a massive integrated system of nerves and hormones directly affecting the trillions of cells composing our bodies, consequently our ability to think and act. The higher frequencies of your Energy Field penetrate your mental realm, conscious and subconscious, to translate into sane thoughts and healthy coordinated physical function. Your mind is by nature openly responsive to higher frequencies. It loves the dance! It is one with the energizing Field, not separate like your TV set that needs to be connected to electricity and aerial/cable to receive transmission. Visualize your mind and body as one permeable filter allowing high frequency broadcasts to flow through, translating them into mental and physical levels. While the source of these broadcasts comes through your own Energy Field they become mixed with other thoughts, feelings, and impulses from visible and invisible worlds around you. Here is where thought forms and feelings from your Field, your source, can begin to integrate with the many influences around you, hopefully resulting in confident orientation and understanding. Such is not possible for your TV set; an electronic receiver that can only transmit broadcasts it receives. If turned on it will express audio and video signals just as they are received whether into a room full of hatred or love, a noisy auto body shop, a store in a shopping mall or in the midst of an earthquake or tidal wave – the broadcast remains unchanged. In other words the transmitter has no choice, no ability to think things through or integrate some of the other factors happening round about. Only one function – *receive and express* – as long as power is turned on and antenna tuned. In contrast, your mental equipment is animated by your living Field and you can choose to express what's coming from that source, parrot what you feel and hear around you or better, integrate the two. This is what it means to be alive and awake as a human, not limited to compulsion from within or knee jerk reactions to what's around you, but to reflect, think and integrate – free to express and act as you choose. We're talking about **your** mind here, a capacity involving brain activity not only working with forms and facts but a facility that includes what we call feeling or emotion. Yes, we have a so-called "left-brained" ability to assess the facts with logic and reason and a "right-brained" ability to feel and intuit the unseen and unknown. These two aspects are often referred to as mind and heart. This level of heart, not distinct from the vascular pump in your chest, refers to your sensitivity to perceive your feelings and to emote – express emotion – a vital part of mental

activity sometimes passed off as "just my emotions". In our western
or developed world we pay homage to rational logical thought when
in fact it never exists without the dimension of feeling or emotion.
Unlike Star Trek's image of Dr. Spock, perhaps revered as the ultimate
scientific "master of logic", it is not possible to hear, hold, or express
a thought devoid of feeling. Love, hatred, fear, respect, resentment,
awe, indifference, excitement, pleasure, compassion etc. are some of
the feeling components under-girding and enveloping your thoughts.
Emotion is the power energizing thought; thoughts never exist alone
without this foundational essence.

One of the greatest assets to clear thinking personally and in
communication with others is the ability to listen. Hearing is not
listening; an electronic recorder hears but doesn't have the ability to
understand; that comes with listening. Under stress from the world
around us plus lack of clarity and integration of our own thoughts and
feelings we may retreat into ourselves, become self-absorbed, causing
our listening ability to shrink. Even when someone is speaking directly
to us we hear only a portion of what they are saying if our thoughts are
directed to an opinion about what they are saying and how we are
going to reply to them. Our insecurity spawns defensiveness so our
inner space is disturbed, distorting even the small portion we hear of
what they're saying if not completely ignoring them and their value as
a person. Much of what passes for communication is about parry and
thrust as though sparring with an opponent. This is both demeaning
and frustrating to the one wanting to commune-icate with us. Everyone
longs to be seen and heard as a valid individual, ultimately a respected
colleague or even a friend. As we find our own footing and balance
within our Field our ability to listen will expand allowing us to be

touched and to touch another – not a physical touch but a feeling one. What are mutual respect and friendship but sharing ideas and points of view on a foundation of two hearts not afraid to meet and hear each other. I'm not speaking about physical intimacy particularly although application will certainly fit. What about the opportunity of building bonds of understanding and respect with people we meet and talk to? The world is full of misunderstanding, prejudice, conflict and war – incomplete communication resulting in senseless destruction. What could happen if people began to honestly listen to one another, build mutual understanding with a passion to work together for the common good? Perhaps it begins with me? The words of a song come to mind, "Let There Be Peace On Earth And Let It Begin With Me!"

Exploring deeper, there are questions inside us about personal destiny and a sense of meaning. What am I here to do with my life? Is there a job description in my soul -- unique qualities and gifts to express? Is it possible I could enhance the collective awareness and well-being of all humankind? Is this hidden sense of destiny compelling me or is that delusion – maybe just philosophical rhetoric? Or was I just a blank slate at birth to fill in what I wanted to do according to what I saw might be pleasing, no doubt swayed by my culture and views espoused by those around me? These are questions to be answered in pursuit of my inherent personal destiny before opportunity passes me by. There are no sadder words than, "what might have been".

The noise of the world around us and our own haunting insecurities are major distractions clouding our vision and our lives. We eventually stop listening, retreating into our defense mechanisms to preserve whatever sanity we can hang on to. We tend to lose contact with what's real in our deeper heart and soul. How do we counter these pressures and come free of limitations in order to hear our unique voice reverberating through our Energy Field? In other words, "How do I become more genuinely me?"

Some have found meditation helpful and there are many forms. Journal writing about experiences, past and present, and exposing hidden feelings can release you from their hold on you into a clearer vision of your real nature. Those experiencing physical releases and growth through Vibrational Healing often find their awareness expanding into an understanding of greater potential in living. Wise counsel may guide us to open deeper understanding of self and heart sensitivity. It is inspiring to read relevant books and converse with people who carry a vision of vibrant wholeness in living.

Speaking of inspiration and personal clarity, my wife and I find an ongoing gift in Avatar. We first attended a Course in the early 1990s shortly after Harry Palmer had launched the program. Avatar outlines a new understanding about and beyond the human mind, how to deal with things in consciousness that are blocking forward movement in one's living experience. On Course are effective exercises to do, that locate transparent or unseen factors from our past programming and indoctrination. These are holding us back and causing difficulties in our lives. The masters and trainers are caring understanding people on hand to assist you to find your unique hidden beliefs, and to show you how to release them so that you can live your life with greater effectiveness and ease. Avatar has grown to over 100,000 participants internationally and the Courses are offered in many languages. We find it nourishing to use the Avatar exercises and tools to participate in a clarification of consciousness and are thrilled with the overall purpose of Avatar, the emergence of an enlightened planetary civilization.

www.avatarepc.com

I enjoy the opportunity within the whole spectrum of living to achieve soft listening and the silent mind. The experience approaches a level of mastery – a genuine person, naturally humble, always willing to learn more through personal introspection, and exercising respect for others with an openness to wise counsel. It involves gaining emotional stability and a clear mind, being sensitive with an open heart to one's personal inner wisdom. Honoring this expanding awareness with the personal opportunity to keep evolving in understanding is the ultimate essence of being responsibly human. Although intricately complex we are wondrously made with the privilege of being a priceless gift to ourselves, an inspiration to others and a positive influence in the overall state of human consciousness. It is a tall and exciting challenge to aspire to mastery. While absolute perfection may never be achieved it's a wonderful experience growing toward it. Here is the excitement of living to the fullest! Here is the ultimate of experiencing ongoing personal vitality.

Epilogue
what about the larger picture?

We've been considering the importance of the Human Energy Field as it relates to you and me – a very personal subject.

Each of us is:

- a complex human entity with an identity unique from other humans
- a body of some trillions of individual cells arranged into many organs and living systems functioning as one coordinated finely tuned organism
- a mental capacity, part conscious with a vast unconscious back-up, involved in the operation of all physical functions, conscious thought, memory and more
- a vast feeling capacity – potentially a humanitarian emotional heart
- an unseen mix of our inherited characteristics as well as personal attitudes we've created about almost everything; likes, dislikes, friends, enemies, experiences we've had and challenges yet to come
- a personal Energy Field we are just becoming acquainted with surrounding, penetrating, activating and monitoring all of the above, carrying the potential of health, sanity, happiness and a sense of meaning.

There are various estimates about the number of cells in our bodies, apparently numbering about 50 trillion individual microscopic cells. Each cell has a specific design, function, a mind of its own and a vital Micro Energy Field monitoring directing and caring for it. Every cell performs its duties over a short life span, dies and is replaced by a new almost identical one. Does that remind you of our lives on earth?

[By the way: a cancer cell is a normal cell not receiving clear guidance from its Field or getting a distorted message from It, thus becoming subject to other distractions affecting its design and function.]

Consider how similar the body of humankind is to our individual bodies. At first glance the world body appears to be larger but isn't that just a matter of perspective? It is now more than 7 billion human beings, much less than the trillions of cells that compose our bodies. Visualize the human world, with you and me as individual cells, all of our Fields enveloped by a Global Human Energy Field that surrounds, penetrates, activates and monitors all of us, potentially as one body of uniquely individual people. Looking at that world now we observe the evidence of destructive interferences to the creative potential within this larger Field. News media reports many of those every day in addition to what we see with our own eyes. Perhaps these glitches are caused by current or historical traumas maintained with persistent conscious and unconscious attitudes governing each and all of us individuals. The resulting dissonance expands from individuals into communities and nations keeping them separate and at odds with one another. Then disputes between neighbors become angry stand-offs, between nations – cold wars, and here and there wars large or small break out and everyone suffers except those that manufacture and distribute weapons of war. Could we diagnose these conflicts as "ill health" cancerous conditions within the larger body of humankind instead of an active state of cooperation and harmony? Some people-cells become parasites, or are born that way, inciting destruction or passively following those that do. If integrity, honesty and compassion were exercised by enough individuals, blind spots and historical animosities could be recognized and released so the potential clarity of The Larger Field could express itself through each person, affecting the leaders of communities and nations? Wouldn't that manifest as peace, a cooperative harmony in expression? Consider the words of John Lenon's song:

Imagine

Imagine there's no heaven
It's easy if you try
No hell below us
Above us only sky
Imagine all the people
Living for today…

Imagine there's no countries
It isn't hard to do
Nothing to kill or die for
And no religion too
Imagine all the people
Living life in peace…

You may say I'm a dreamer
But I'm not the only one
I hope someday you'll join us
And the world will be as one

Imagine no possessions
I wonder if you can
No need for greed or hunger
A brotherhood of man
Imagine all the people
Sharing all the world…

You may say I'm a dreamer
But I'm not the only one
I hope someday you'll join us
And the world will be one

What would it take to reach that state of balance/ harmony/ oneness/ peace? That is a naturally inherent potential in any creative body, within itself and in its interaction with others. It is our challenge personally to rise to that level of integration. We can choose a personal intention to peel away the subtle layers of being a victim, always with someone else to blame. Undertaking this personal work with constant vigilance, one moment at a time, one can transcend feeling victimized to a state of being responsible in any circumstance. Doing so we become the leaven in the lump, a radiant catalyst in the world we live in, quietly or in an overt way. Who knows where that would take us, you – me – others? Unimagined possibilities can open when we acknowledge and begin to understand our own Energy Field, take the steps to uncover the blockages we're carrying around and learn to clarify them. So doing we assume responsibility for our personal presence and extend a positive creative influence into the larger collective human field. Are we victims of mother nature "miserable sinners" as it were, or is the Field of this planet desperate to feel that humankind is in balance extending a positive vibratory influence so everything can continue to evolve. Indeed our Energy Field has been too long a forgotten asset.

It's been a pleasure to share with you experiences and thoughts about The Human Energy Field. For sure the last word has not been spoken about this vast and vital Field, the source of its wisdom and our limitless opportunities within it.

www.ronald-healing.com

The End

Bibliography
Your Incredible Energy Field

Bly, Robert (1988) *A Little Book On The Human Shadow*, Harper San Francisco

Cousins, Norman (1981) *Anatomy of an Illness as Perceived by the Patient*, Bantam Books, New York

Cousins, Norman (1983) *The Healing Heart: Antidotes to Panic and Helplesssness*, Norton, New York

Cousins, Norman (1989) *Head First: The Biology of Hope*, E.P. Dutton, New York

Davies, Brenda (2000) *The 7 Healing Chakras: Unlocking Your Body's Energy Centers*, Ulysses Press, Berkeley, CA

Diamond, John (1979) *Your Body Doesn't Lie*, Axis Publishing, Great Britain

Evans, Michael & Rodger, Iain (1992) *Anthroposophical Medicine: Healing For Body, Soul & Spirit*, Thorsons-Harper Collins Publishers, London

Franz M. L., C.G. Jung: *His Myth In Our Time*

Gerber, Richard (1988) *Vibrational Medicine: New Choices For Healing Ourselves*, Bear & Company, Santa Fe, New Mexico

Hawkins, David R. (2002) *Power vs Force*, Hay House, Carlsbad, CA

Hillman James, (1996) *The Soul's Code: In Search of Character and Calling*, Random House Inc. New York and Toronto

Hollis, James (2005) *Finding Meaning In The Second Half Of Life; How To Really Grow Up*, Gotham Books(Penguin Group) New York

Hunt, Valerie (1996) *Infinite Mind: Science of the Human Vibrations of Consciousess*, Malibu Publishing Co.

Johnson, Grant (2004) quotation from *Vibrational Vitality*, by Ronald Polack

Jung C.G., *Memory, Dreams, Reflection*

Kuhl, David (2002) *What Dying People Want*, Anchor Canada (Random House)

Leadbetter, C.W. (1927, 1972) *The Chakras*, Theosophical Publishing House, Wheaton, Illinois

Legato, Marianne, Why Men Never Remember and Women Never Forget

Lennon, John – Song: *Imagine*

Mate, Gabor (2003) *When the Body Says No*, Alfred A. Knopf, Canada

McTaggart, Lynne (2002) *The Field: The Quest for the Secret Force of The Universe*, Harper Collins Publishers, New York, NY

Moore, Robert and Gillette, Douglas (1991), *King, Warrior, Magician, Lover*, HarperSanFrancisco

Myss, Carolyn (1997) *Why People Don't Heal And How They Can*, Harmony, CA

Nuland, Sherwin B (1997) *The Wisdom Of the Body*, Alfred A. Knop, Canada

Palmer , Harry (2005) *Living Deliberately*, Star's Edge International, Altamonte Springs, Florida

Peale, Norman Vincent (1952) *The Power Of Positive Thinking*, Prentice Hall, New York

Perte, Candice (1997) *Molecules Of Emotion*, Touchstone, New York

Sheldrake, Rupert (2003) *The Sense of Being Stared At* and *Dogs That Know When Their Owners Are Coming Home*, Crown Publishers, New York

Siegel, Bernie S. (1986) *Love, Medicine, & Miracles; Lessons Learned About Self-Healing From a Surgeon's Experience with Exceptional Patients*, Harper & Rowe Publishers Inc. New York

Strang, Virgil (1985) *Essential Principles of Chiropractic*, Palmer College of Chiropractic, Davenport, Iowa

Suzuki, David (1997) *The Sacred Balance*, Greystone Books, Vancouver, Canada

Tolle, Eckhart (1997) *The Power Of Now,* Namaste Publishing, Vancouver, Canada

Sir Laurence Van der Post, *A Walk With A White Bushman,* Random House

Verny, Thomas (1981) *The Secret Life Of The Unborn Child*

Weil, Andrew (1995) *Spontaneous Healing,* Ballantine Books (Random House) Canada